Become a Reiki Master

Usui Holy Fire Reiki Level III/ART & Master Training Manual

Adrian Campbell, PhD

Copyright ©2025 by Adrian Campbell, PhD
Cover and internal design by Adrian Campbell, PhD

All rights reserved. No part of this book may be reproduced in any form or by any electronic or mechanical means including information storage and retrieval systems - except in the case of brief quotations embodied in critical articles or reviews - without permission in writing from Adrian Campbell, PhD.

Published by Adrian Campbell, PhD
www.EnergeticPsyche.com

Table of Contents

Chapter 1: Setting a Foundation 1

    Reiki Ideals 2

    Energy Healing 3

    Reiki Energy Healing 6

        The History & Evolution of Reiki 6

        Different Levels of Reiki 8

Chapter 2: Usui Holy Fire Reiki Level III/Advanced Reiki Training (ART) 14

    Reiki Level III/Advanced Reiki Training (ART) 15

    The Healing Power of Crystals 15

    Using Reiki with Crystals 17

        Cleaning & Clearing Stones 17

        Creating Crystal "Healing Bundles" 18

    Creating Crystal Grids 21

    Exploring the Chakra System 25

        Working with the Energetic Body 26

    Reiki Master Symbol – Dai Ko Myo 29

    Understanding Reiki Attunements 31

        The Attunement Cleansing Process 32

    Reiki Healing Attunements 33

        Giving a Reiki Healing Attunement 34

        Healing Attunement Preparation Script 35

        Dai Ko Myo Healing Attunement 37

        Dai Ko Myo Healing Attunement Quick Guide 44

Chapter 3: Usui Holy Fire Reiki Master 48

Becoming a Reiki Master 49

Usui Holy Fire Reiki 49

Reiki Level I, II, III/ART Attunements 53

Giving Attunements to Groups vs. Individuals 54

Usui Holy Fire Reiki Healing Attunement 55

Usui Holy Fire Healing Attunement Quick Guide 62

Usui Holy Fire Reiki I Attunement 65

Usui Holy Fire Reiki I Attunement Quick Guide 73

Usui Holy Fire Reiki II Attunement 75

Usui Holy Fire Reiki II Attunement Quick Guide 83

Usui Holy Fire Reiki III/ART Attunement 85

Usui Holy Fire Reiki III/ART Attunement Quick Guide 93

Usui Holy Fire Reiki Master Ignitions 95

Meditations vs Guided Experiences 95

Usui Holy Fire Reiki Master Pre-Ignition 97

Usui Holy Fire Reiki Master Ignition I 101

Usui Holy Fire Reiki Master Ignition II 104

Chapter 4: The Basics of Teaching Reiki 108

Teaching Tips & Tidbits 110

Setting Your Fees 111

Finding Class Space 112

Equipment Needed 113

Websites & Marketing 114

Insurance 115

Class Registration & Enrollment 116

Appendix A: Reiki Symbols 118

Reiki Level II Symbols 119

Choku Rei 120

Sei Heki 121

Hon Sha Ze Sho Nen 122

Dai Ko Myo 123

Holy Fire 124

Appendix B: Reiki Class Outlines 126

Standard Reiki Class Outlines 127

    Class Prep Email 129

    Usui Holy Fire Reiki Level I Class Outline (8hrs) 131

    Usui Holy Fire Reiki Level II Class Outline (8 hrs) 136

    Usui Holy Fire Reiki Level I/II Class Outline (2 Days) 140

    Usui Holy Fire Reiki Level III/ART Class Outline (8hrs) 146

    Usui Holy Fire Reiki Level III/ART & Reiki Master Class Outline (3 Days) 150

Appendix C: Guided Meditations & Experiences 160

Holy Love Experience – Winding River 161

Holy Love Experience - Waterfall 163

Chapter 1

Setting a Foundation

The Reiki Ideals

Just for today,
I will let go of worry

Just for today,
I will let go of anger

Just for today, I will thanks for
my many blessings

Just for today,
I will do my work honestly

Just for today,
I will be kind to my neighbor and
all living things

If you are reading this book as a Level II or higher Reiki Practitioner, the information in this first section will seem like a refresher. However, with the multitude of ways people are getting their Reiki training these days, we need to be careful making assumptions as to what people know and what they do not. With that in mind, the following section was written as a way to create a mutually shared foundation of knowledge with which to experience the rest of this book's teachings from. Please keep and use what you like, and feel free to leave what doesn't align with your practice or beliefs.

Energy Healing

Everything is energy… whether animate or not, our entire world is made up of atoms and stardust, held together by varying frequencies to form the images we interact with in the world. What makes living beings different is the addition of a special form of energy, called Life Force Energy. This energy is widely known throughout the world as Chi, Ki, or Prana, and flows through us like a river, ensuring that our energy doesn't become stagnant, or still.

Unfortunately, as many of us know, life isn't always easy and it's a given that we will experience different types of physical, mental, or emotional injuries throughout our lifetimes. These injuries manifest not only in our physical bodies, but also energetically in the form of energetic blocks, creating pebbles, rocks, and boulders in the river of our Life Force Energy.

Energetic blocks negatively impact our well-being by restricting the flow of our Life Force Energy. These energetic blocks can manifest as symptoms of dis-ease, in the physical, mental/emotional, and energetic body. Depending on the severity of the injury, and the length of time we endure its affects, our Life Force Energy may be reduced to a trickle, or in some cases, these energetic blocks can be large enough to completely stop the flow.

When the flow of our Life Force Energy is interrupted, the way we interact with the world changes, it becomes distorted as our system tries to adjust to the interference. Over time if the blocks are not healed, we create new patterns of functioning, psychologically, emotionally, and physically, which only act to reinforce the block and continue to limit flow.

Think about the impact of a broken ankle… physically this manifests with a broken bone, symptoms of swelling, the inability to use that area of the body, an adjustment in how the entire body will be able to move for a period of time, and of course, physical pain. Mentally and emotionally the injury may create feelings of frustration, anger, sadness, and more, depending on how the injury occurred and how long it will take to heal. Energetically, a severe broken ankle can create a blockage in the flow of Life Force Energy, restricting flow to the foot, which if not acknowledged can lead to lasting issues in that area of the body, even once the ankle has physically healed.

Energy healing works through focused intention to remove these blocks, so that our Life Force Energy can flow freely again, allowing us to heal. In the case of the broken ankle, energy healing can assist in maintaining a healthy flow of energy to the foot while the ankle heals, as well as encouraging healing to occur in the area of the broken bone.

Anyone can access energy healing to help themselves or others, as we are all made up of energy and have the power of intention available to us. However, depending on your current energetic state, working with your own energy may cause more harm than good, and over time using your own energy to heal can be exhausting.

To avoid wearing yourself out by using your own energy, there are several other forms of energy healing available which allow you to work with the source of Life Force Energy, rather than your own. Through use of some of these other forms of energy healing, such as Reiki, you have the ability to help yourself and others without becoming depleted.

Reiki Energy Healing

Reiki energy is a specific form of energy, considered to be a direct connection to the source of Life Force Energy. The term Reiki is made up of two Japanese words; Rei meaning "Universal" and Ki meaning "Life Force Energy". Out of the different types of energy healing available, the International Center of Reiki Training (ICRT) believes Reiki to be of the highest frequency and to be guided by spiritual consciousness.

When working with Reiki energy you are connected to the source of Life Force Energy, a spiritually guided energy which when invited to, can remove any blocks that may be present in yourself or others. Reiki Practitioners do not heal, but rather act as a channel for the Reiki energy, allowing it to flow through them to another. Because of this, the Reiki Practitioner's own energies will never be depleted, but rather, they will be continually refreshed as they receive a session every time they give one.

As Reiki is guided by spiritual consciousness it will never do any harm and will never go against anyone's will. Reiki energy will always act in a way that is in the best interest of the person receiving the Reiki energy.

The History & Evolution of Reiki

Reiki originated in Japan, discovered by Usui Sensei on Mt. Kumara in 1922. Usui Sensei had gone to Mt. Kumara to meditate and gain clarity in his life. He spent 21 days fasting in a cave and on the 21st day a white light entered the crown of his head bringing the clarity he desired, along with a rejuvenation in his spirit. During Usui Sensei's rush down the mountain to share about his experience, he tripped over a rock, injuring his toe. When he put his hands to his foot, the pain subsided and the injury was healed. Astonished he continued back into town and began to share what he had learned during his experience on Mt. Kumara.

In the four years before he passed in 1926, Usui Sensei opened several clinics, trained over 2,000 students, and received an award from the Japanese government for the healing work he did after the devastating earthquake in 1923. It was through two of his students, a naval medical doctor named Chujiro Hayashi and a Hawaiian woman named Hawayo Takata (often referred to as Mrs. Takata) the practice of Reiki evolved and spread throughout Japan and Hawaii, until its growth was unfortunately cut short due to World War II.

Mrs. Takata had brought Reiki back from Japan to Hawaii in 1937, but once Japan joined World War II, the stigma attached to anything considered Japanese inhibited the practice from gaining popularity. She continued to practice and train others, but westernized the methodology and would not allow written notes to be taken. In addition, Mrs. Takata charged $10,000 for her Reiki Master training, which made it almost impossible for the practice to spread. In the early 1980s, one of Mrs. Takata's students decided to train her own students for more reasonable amounts of money, opening the path for Reiki to begin to spread more easily.

Since the very beginning of Reiki's introduction to the world through Usui Sensei, the practice of Reiki has continued to grow and evolve. Many teachers over the years have followed their inner guidance, adding additional healing modalities and symbols, channeling Reiki energies from specific guides, and adjusting rituals to fit their personal practices and beliefs. There is no one right way to practice Reiki, rather, it is more important that you find the way that best suits you.

This book in particular shares information based on learning experiences gained working with multiple teachers of varying backgrounds and affiliations. The symbols, techniques, and rituals shared here, have been honed into a specific practice developed over the past decade by Dr. Adrian Campbell. The master symbols used are Dai Ko Myo and Holy Fire, and the attunement processes described follow the teaching and spiritual guidance received by Dr. Campbell' multiple certifications as a Reiki Master, and the experience she shared in 2014 with William Rand of the ICRT, when he decided to channel Usui Holy Fire Reiki in a class for the first time.

Different Levels of Reiki

Though there are many different types of Reiki trainings and lineages around the world, the levels shared below are those which have become fairly standard and are used by the majority of teachers in the U.S. But again, just because a Reiki training program doesn't fit the structure described in this book, doesn't make it wrong. If you feel called to experience or teach Reiki in a different way, feel free to explore that.

Reiki Level I

Reiki Level I is the most basic form of Reiki and the lowest level of Reiki energy. As you go up in levels the frequency of the Reiki you are attuned to rises. Reiki I involves the fundamentals and history of Reiki, and how to give self-sessions. Classes can range from 4-8 hours, and can be taught individually or in combination with Reiki Level II over a weekend.

Reiki Level II

Reiki Level II teaches the first three Reiki symbols and their uses, including the Power symbol (Choku Rei), the Mental/Emotional symbol (Sei Heki), and the Distance Reiki symbol (Hon Sha Ze Sho Nen). This level of Reiki teaches a multitude of ways that Reiki can be used in practical everyday applications and is often where students begin to develop a deeper relationship with Reiki energy. This is also the level that teaches the Reiki Practitioner how to practice Reiki on others using intuition, standard hand placements, and distance techniques.

Reiki Level III/ART

Reiki Level III, also known as ART (Advanced Reiki Training) was originally part of Reiki Master training, but broke off to accommodate individuals that wanted to deepen their Reiki practice with an attunement to the Reiki Master symbol, but had no intention of teaching others.

In Reiki Level III the students are given the Reiki Master symbol and attuned to that level of frequency. Depending on the Reiki Master teaching the class other healing techniques, such as moving meditations, working with crystals, aura clearing, etc., may also be shared.

This level is typically taught as the first day of Usui Holy Fire Reiki Master training, as the ignition process for Usui Holy Fire Reiki takes three days, with the first ignition given during the Level III/ART class. However, it can be taught as a stand alone class.

Reiki Master

Reiki Master is the final level of Reiki training and all one needs to become a Reiki Master and Teacher. However, there are many individuals who choose to complete multiple Reiki Master trainings, often benefiting from their experience with teachers of different lineages, as the training material and attunement processes can differ widely across different styles. Learning Reiki from multiple teachers is always encouraged and at the level of Reiki Master it can be helpful in gathering different techniques to develop your own unique practice.

As mentioned earlier, the style taught in this book is in alignment with Usui Holy Fire Reiki Master training, which differs from the more traditional style of Usui

Reiki Master training. Where the traditional Usui Reiki Master training involves an attunement and multiple additional symbols to be learned, Usui Holy Fire Reiki Master training involves a multi-day ignition process, only one additional symbol, and significantly reduced ritual around the process of connecting to spiritual consciousness. These differences make Usui Holy Fire Reiki a great option for those looking for simplicity and a more directly personal experience.

During Usui Holy Fire Reiki Master training the students are connected to spiritual consciousness at the highest frequency of Reiki. They are taught how to give attunements for levels I, II, III/ART, and the ignitions necessary for Usui Holy Fire Reiki Master.

This book (as part of Level III/ART) also teaches how to give Reiki Healing Attunements, which use the higher frequency Reiki attunement energy to help heal a block or specific issue in a client.

The symbol for Reiki is in Japanese Kanji and depicts the heavens above, the Earth below, and the human healer as the in between.

Chapter 2

Reiki Level III/ Advanced Reiki Training (ART)

Reiki Level III/Advanced Reiki Training (ART)

This level of Reiki was never taught by Usui Sensei or Mrs. Takata, it was developed by her students for individuals that were interested in furthering their relationship with Reiki energy, but who didn't necessarily want to teach others. Originally the class consisted of learning the Reiki Master Symbol, Dai Ko Myo, becoming attuned to it, and time to practice using it on others in a Reiki session.

Over the years different Reiki teachers have added other techniques to the Level III/ART class based on their personal learnings and experience. What a Level III/ART student learns depends highly on who an individual decides to do their training with.

The Reiki Level III/ART training taught in this book includes a cultivated set of practices standardly used for over a decade by Dr. Campbell as both a Reiki Practitioner and Reiki Teacher.

The Healing Power of Crystals

Crystals hold two types of power, innate power and assigned power. Their innate power stems from their geophysical properties and does not shift or change based on location, culture, or use. Their assigned power, however, is not necessarily static, and may change depending on who is using it and how.

For example, Rose Quartz has similar physical properties to Clear Quartz, which allows it to absorb and store energy, as well as any intentions associated with it.

Over the years, starting as far back as 7000 BC, Rose Quartz has been used as a form of jewelry or talisman. Romans used it as a seal of ownership, Egyptians believed it could prevent aging, and the early civilizations of the Americas believed it to be a "love stone", which is primarily what it is known for now.

As each of these civilizations attached their own specific meanings to Rose Quartz, they also energetically assigned the type of power it would emit. These power assignments are reinforced through cultural beliefs, and over time become a part of the energetic makeup of the stone.

This day and age, Rose Quartz is still commonly known as a "love stone", one that is related to the energies of the heart chakra, including compassion and self-love. If you meditate with Rose Quartz you can sense these energies, because they have been reinforced through belief and intention over thousands of years.

Now, all that being said… there are those who believe that stones come out of the earth with a set purpose ascribed to them by source, as well as inherent metaphysical properties that we can all use for our benefit.

Lumerian Crystal Healers believe that crystals, stones, and rocks (all the same thing really, just in different forms) are all an extension of Mother Earth and should be treated as a type of sentient being with needs and wants, just like a plant might have. Many different stones have a sense of purpose in their life and want to help just as much as we do. To get the most out of your experience working with stones try to get to know them, spend time with them, create a relationship with them, like you would a new friend. It is through relationship with them that a partnership can be formed and you will be able to do the best work.

When you choose a stone for a specific purpose, try to keep an open mind. Be sure to visit a shop that you feel good about being in (vibe is important!), flow some Reiki and let your hands hover over the different stones. See which ones you are guided to work with, take a few minutes to hold them, resonate with them, *talk* with them. Don't limit yourself to stones that some book told you to use, just go out there and say Hi, then listen for who says Hi back.

Using Reiki with Crystals

Clear quartz is THE stone to use in energy healing. As mentioned above, its physical properties allow it to absorb and store energy, then slowly emit that energy and intention back into the world over a sustained period of time. Basically, quartz was *made* for energy work.

When you charge a quartz crystal it will absorb the Reiki energy from your palms, as well as any intention you send along with the energy. For example, if you wanted to charge a stone to help you focus more throughout the day, you would begin flowing Reiki and then state your intention, as you would with any session, and then hold the stone between your palms and flow Reiki directly into the stone.

Some people find it helpful to create a mantra or positive statement to repeat as they flow Reiki into their stone. For the example above, something like this would work, "I am focused and calm, I am focused and calm, I am focused and calm".

It is recommended that you continue to charge your stone for as long as you'd like, but generally no less than 2-3 minutes. The longer you charge the stone, the more energy it will store. The bigger the stone the greater the capacity for energy storage and the longer you will need to charge it.

Cleaning & Clearing Stones

There are several different reasons why you would want to energetically clean or clear a stone. Maybe you want to use a stone that has been in use for a different reason, maybe it's going from one healing bundle to another, perhaps it was part of a grid, or you acquired it from sources unknown and just want to be sure you get a clean energetic start.

You can do this by burying it in the dirt (usually for a couple days), give it a bath (be sure it can handle water, Selenite for example will dissolve), or use Reiki. To use Reiki to clear a stone you simply flow Reiki into the stone with the intention to clean and clear the stone. You just want to be sure that whatever energy you put into it previously has been cleared before you charge it with something new.

As mentioned in the previous section. Stones are sentient in a way and will often share how they would like to be cleaned, so it isn't a bad idea to ask the stone which they would prefer. Don't question it too much, just go with your gut feeling, trust yourself, you'll know.

An additional practice, which isn't always necessary, but is always helpful, is sending Reiki healing energy to the source of the stone. You can do this using distance Reiki to connect to where the stone was extracted from the earth, filling the hole left behind with love and gratitude. This can help to release any traumas that may have stuck with the stone based on how they were extracted from Mother Earth.

Creating Crystal "Healing Bundles"

The simplest way to use stones in conjunction with your Reiki practice is to create "healing bundles". Healing bundles are a nifty way to keep your intentions in one place, and when carried with you, they act as a physical reminder and energetic reinforcer, keeping you aligned consciously and unconsciously with your goals. You can make them for yourself, your loved ones, as well as your students and clients. Once they are made up they can be put in a pocket, purse, glove compartment, backpack, or even under a pillow.

To create a healing bundle, determine who the healing is for, what intention you would like to send, and then spend some time choosing which stones you think would best support this intention. To put it together you just need a little bag, it can be a fancy velvet bag or a simple mesh bag, but please avoid plastic if possible.

In a typical healing bundle, there is one quartz crystal, two additional stones that support the intention, and a small piece of paper with the mantra/intention/affirmation written on it. On the following page is an example of a healing bundle created to support someone experiencing low self-esteem.

To charge the bundle, you will begin to flow Reiki as you would for any other session, then place the bundle between your hands and repeat your mantra while flowing Reiki into the bundle. Continue to do this for a minimum of 2-3 minutes, and then you can give the bundle to the person, place it on your altar, or carry it with you. If you have access to it, it is a good idea to re-charge it daily as a part of your morning practice.

Creating a Healing Bundle

Clear Quartz to act as the primary crystal which will hold your Reiki energy and intention

Carnelian for courage. This stone was often worn on the armor of warriors in battle.

A note writing out the mantra to repeat while charging the stones

Sara, you are amazing and have the courage to achieve anything you put your mind to

Rose Quartz for Self-Love, Respect & Compassion

Creating Crystal Grids

Crystal grids are another great way to work with stones and Reiki energy. Once charged with an intention they will continue to hold and radiate that intention out into the world for as long as the charge of energy lasts. Just like the healing bundles, you can create grids for yourself, your loved ones, as well as your students and clients.

There are many ways to use crystal grids to support Reiki energy healing. Think of anything you would direct Reiki energy towards, and chances are you can use a grid to support it.

Here are a few ideas to get you started:

- Manifesting abundance
- Sending healing energy to others
- Support of an intention or goal
- Attracting a certain type of person or energy into your life
- Increased focus
- Protection for your home or others
- Healing energy to support personal growth
- Courage for new pursuits
- Sending healing energy to world crises
- Sending energy into the future for an upcoming meeting or event
- Sending Reiki into the past to support healing of previous injuries

To create a simple crystal grid, you can start with 6, 9, or 12 quartz points and a center stone of your choosing. You can scale the grid out in size, just be sure to maintain symmetry. The size of the stones will determine the amount of energy the grid can hold and distribute, as well as how long the energy will last. Grids can be the size of your palm, or the size of a room, but try not to get caught up on the size, just know the smaller it is the more often you will have to charge it. It is also worth noting that the bigger the grid gets, the more expensive it gets, and these grids can get up there in price pretty quickly. If you plan to build a lot of grids, remember that it is OK to reuse stones, just be sure to clean them before moving them to a new grid.

The quartz points are the stones that will absorb, hold, and transmit the energy you infuse them with, and the center stone should be a stone in alignment with your intentions. For example, the image on the following page shows a light blue Angelite center stone, so this grid could be used to support throat chakra healing or to help one better connect with their higher self. The size of the center stone should align with the size of your quartz points.

Once the grid is charged it will continue to emit your intentions to the universe as long as it stays charged. How often you re-charge your grid will depend on the size of the stones and the length of your initial charging. I recommend checking in with it daily, perhaps as a part of your daily practice.

To Charge a Crystal Grid

1. Set up the stones on your grid like the one in the picture.

2. Take a moment to get your Reiki energy flowing and draw any symbols over the grid you would like, remembering to push each of them in three times.

3. Beginning at the center of the grid, use your whole hand, middle finger slightly lowered as a "pointer", to draw Reiki energy over the stones. Follow the pattern in the drawing beginning with #1.

4. As you trace Reiki energy over the stones, be sure to repeat you intention, as you are charging the stones with every pass.

5. Make a minimum of three rounds, and once complete, hold your hands over the grid (or draw a power symbol over the top of the grid), and repeat "I seal this grid with Love and Light" three times.

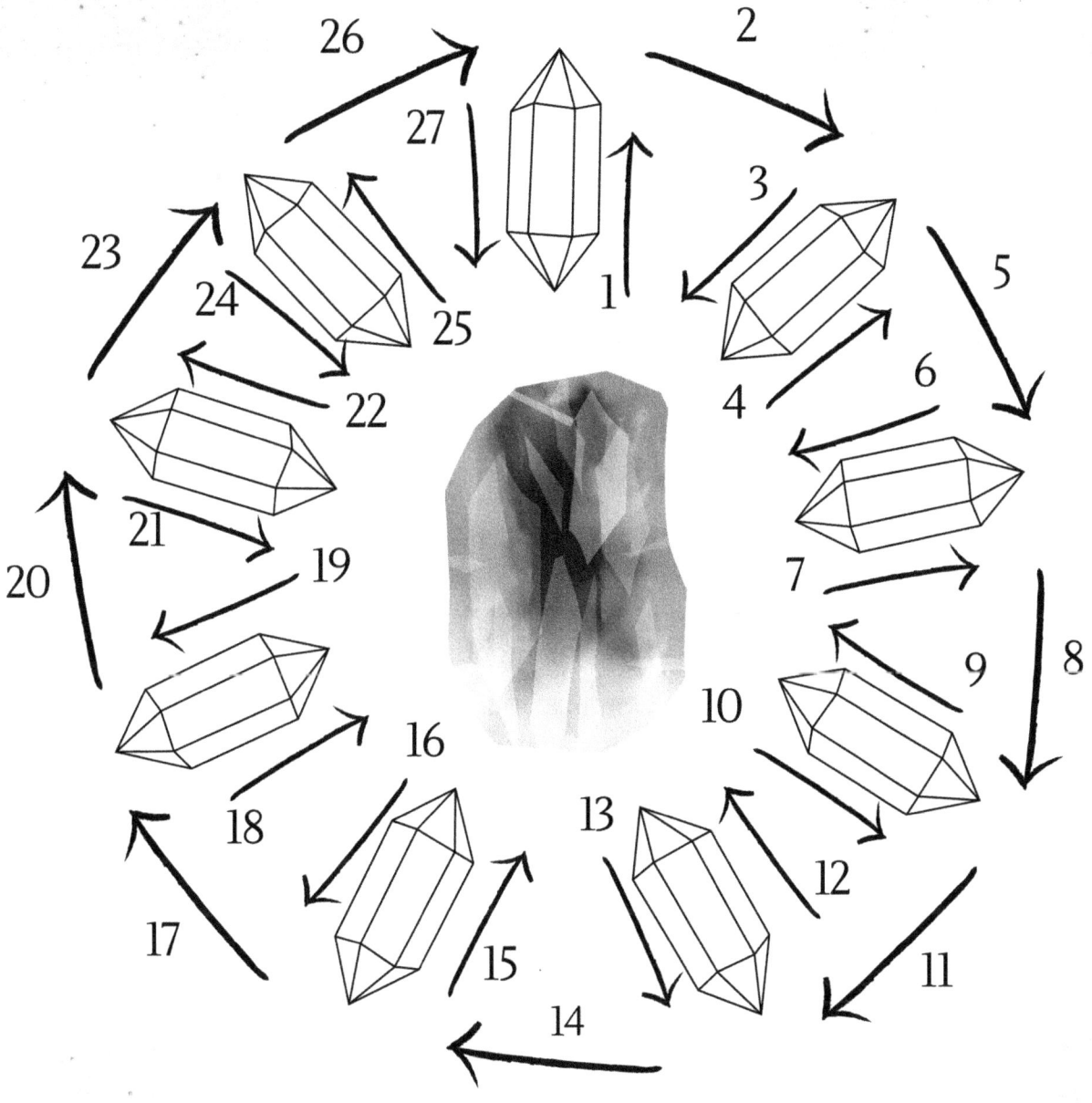

Exploring the Chakra System

A strong understanding of the chakra system isn't necessary to practice Reiki, however it can be helpful, as well as empowering, to understand the make-up of the energetic body. Through a greater understanding of the chakra system we can better identify ways to support the healing created by Reiki energy. As a practitioner and teacher, this knowledge can help you empower your clients and students to support their own healing through activities associated with specific chakras.

The chakra system is the metaphorical bridge between consciousness and matter, it affects our physical being (breathing, heart rate, and metabolism) just as emotions do. The status of our chakra system directly affects the way we receive and interpret information, changing how we interact with the world.

There are seven major chakras, each of which represents a specific type of energy.

1	Root/Base	Survival/Grounding/Prosperity
2	Sacral	Emotions/Sexuality/Family/Feminine
3	Solar Plexus	Power/Autonomy/Will/Masculine
4	Heart	Compassion/Self Love
5	Throat	Self-Expression/Communication
6	Brow/Third Eye	Intuition/Creativity
7	Crown	Consciousness/Spirit

Too often the chakras are viewed as discrete components which can be worked with individually, but this cannot be further from the truth. All the chakras work together in a holistic manner to maintain balance throughout the energetic system. When one chakra is out of balance, the entire system is affected.

The lower half of the system (chakras 1-3) focus on the physical realities of our existence, and the upper half of the system (chakras 5-7) focus on more ethereal and imaginative states. Chakra 4 connects the upper and lower halves of the system, putting love and compassion at the center of all things.

It is important that neither the upper nor lower half of the system is given preference, but rather, one should strive to bring the entire system into balance.

Working with the Energetic Body

As the chakra system maps onto both the mind and body, it can be accessed by both, creating multiple ways to work with the chakra system to heal energetic imbalances.

The chart on the next page has a few specific ways to work with each chakra. No one method is better than the other, but some will resonate more than others, depending on the individual.

If you would like to learn more about working with the chakra system, check out Dr. Campbell's book "Explore Your Chakra System", a 200+ page workbook exploring each of the seven major chakras in-depth, as well as their typical causes of dis-ease and how best to heal them. It provides an insightful journey through your own energetic system and is a wonderful resource for anyone working energetically with clients or students.

#	Name	Color	Crystal	Essential Oil	Nutrition	Activity
1	Root/Base	Red	Hematite, Bloodstone, Red Jasper, Carnelian, Garnet	Cedarwood, Patchouli, Vetiver, Spruce	Red foods – apples, raspberries, kidney beans, tomatoes, strawberries, pepper, beets	Earthing, dancing to a strong beat, drumming, being in nature
2	Sacral	Orange	Red and brown aventurine, red garnet, red jasper, carnelian	Orange, neroli, jasmine, rosewood, clary sage	Almonds, papaya, passion fruit, pumpkin, orange, coconut	Being in water, creative activities, dancing to fluid music
3	Solar Plexus	Yellow	Topaz, citrine, amber, tiger's eye	Lemongrass, fennel, coriander, lime, myrrh, lemon	Yellow foods – corn, squash, pineapples, peppers, brown rice, oats, ginger, turmeric	Affirmations to boost confidence, "baby step" challenges, warrior yoga poses, laugh
4	Heart	Green	Malachite, jade, green tourmaline, emerald, peridot	Ylang ylang, rose, jasmine, pine, rosewood	Green foods – spinach, kale, chard, lettuce	Loving Kindness Meditation, volunteer, gratitude practices
5	Throat	Turquoise	Turquoise, blue agate, lapis, aquamarine, sodalite	Rosemary, lime, sage, cedarwood, champa	Blue foods – currants, blackberries, blueberries, dragon fruit, kelp, wheatgrass, mushrooms	Singing, repeating mantras, chanting, journaling, vow of silence
6	Brow/Third Eye	Indigo	Lapis, indigo, sodalite, sapphire, blue aventurine	Geranium, jasmine, basil, lavender, rosemary	Purple foods – figs, raisins, eggplant, purple potatoes, prunes	Daydream, imagine the life you'd like to create, connect with your guides
7	Crown	Violet	Amethyst, selenite, clear quartz	Sandalwood, saffron, lotus, jasmine	Fasting - nourish with prayer and meditation	Connect with spirit through prayer or meditation

* Note that none of this information should be used to replace any medical, dietary, or mental health related treatments without the consent of your professional wellness care team.

Reiki Master Symbol – Dai Ko Myo

Similar to the distance symbol, the Reiki Master symbol, Dai Ko Myo, is also Japanese Kanji, a form of written language that uses characters versus letters to symbolize different meanings. Because of the symbolic nature of Kanji, the meaning of Dai Ko Myo can be translated in a few different ways.

When used within the context of Reiki, the most common translation is "Great Shining Light" or "Great Enlightenment". In eastern philosophies Dai Ko Myo is understood to mean "treasure house of the great beaming light" and represents a connection to the Universe's essence within us.

The ICRT believes that this symbol was not actually used by Usui Sensei but was later added to the practice of Reiki by Mrs. Takata or Dr. Hayashi. Those who have worked with the symbol have shared a feeling of deep inner connection to their Higher Self and Inner Teacher or the Reiki Master within.

Dai Ko Myo is a higher frequency than the level II Reiki symbols, and as such feels more intense energetically. Concentrating or meditating with Dai Ko Myo can help you connect more easily to the universal energies you hold within, helping you realize your true potential here on Earth.

Similar to Choku Rei, Dai Ko Myo can also act as a boost of sorts for other symbols. It is helpful to use Dai Ko Myo as you would Choku Rei during sessions or other types of Reiki work to help enhance the energy of the other symbols you use. Simply use it before you apply any others, and it will enhance the energy of those symbols.

Dai Ko Myo

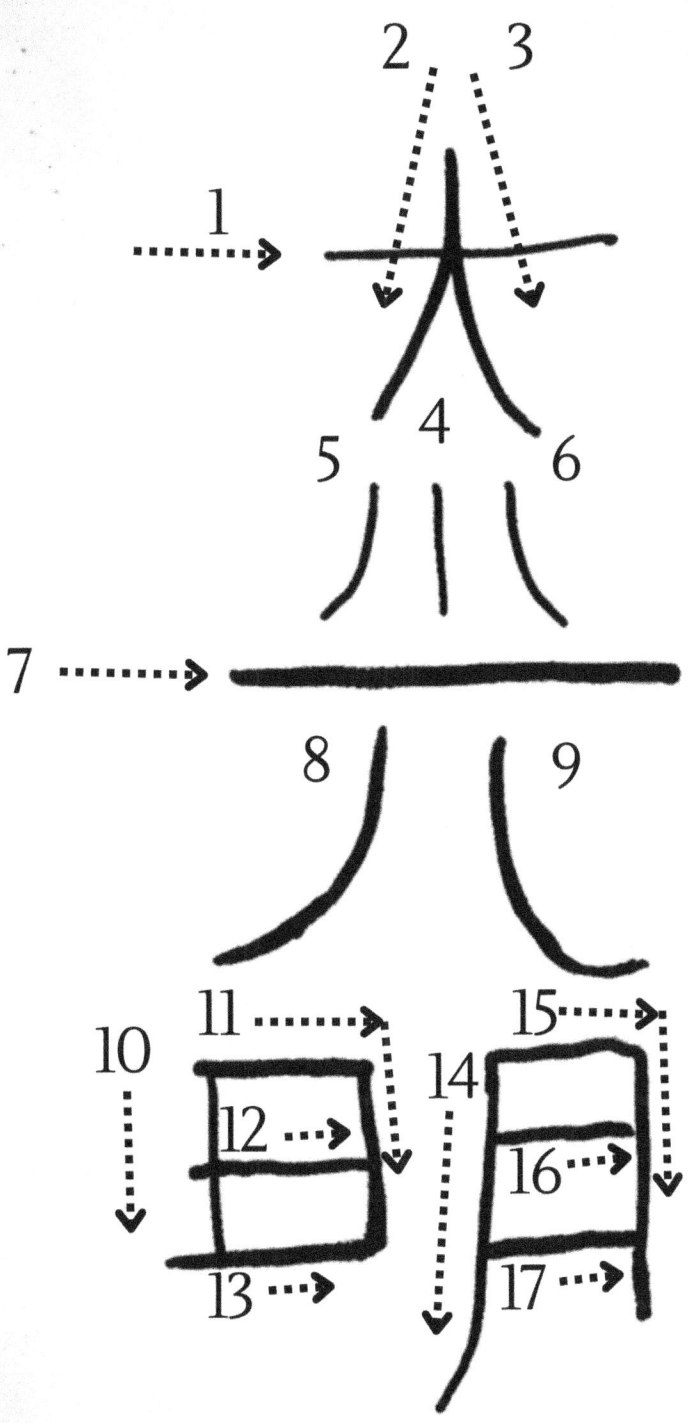

Understanding Reiki Attunements

Reiki attunements are sacred spiritual initiations performed by a Reiki Master for their students or clients. Though it is true that we all have access to Life Force Energy, we only have access to it at a specific frequency. The frequency of Reiki energy is higher than our normal frequency, and each new level of Reiki connects the Practitioner to a higher level of energy.

Reiki Master is the highest energetic frequency within the practice of Reiki, and once you are attuned to that level you have the ability to perform attunements for others.

During an attunement, the Reiki Master holds space energetically, flowing Reiki with the intention to raise the frequency of the student to a specific level of Reiki. The attunement process is like an introduction made by the Reiki Master, between the new Practitioner and the new frequency of Reiki Energy.

As mentioned earlier, the style of attunement taught in this book is in alignment with the original Usui Holy Fire Reiki Master training, which differs from the more traditional style of Usui Reiki Master training. Where the traditional Usui Reiki Master training involves an attunement and multiple additional symbols to be learned, Holy Fire Reiki Master training involves a multi-day ignition process, only one additional symbol, and significantly reduced ritual around the process of connecting to spiritual consciousness. These differences make Usui Holy Fire Reiki a great option for those looking for simplicity and a more directly personal experience.

It is important to note that though the Reiki Master process is different for Holy Fire, the symbols given to the students and the information taught for levels I-III is the same in both Usui Holy Fire Reiki and Usui Reiki.

The Attunement Cleansing Process

During the attunement process the new frequency of energy, led by spiritual consciousness, enters the student and makes necessary accommodations or adjustments in the new Practitioner's energetic body and consciousness, to allow the Practitioner the ability to channel Reiki energy. This process looks and feels different for each person and at each level of Reiki energy

Some students report mystical experiences such as personal messages from guides and loved ones, visions, increased psychic abilities, past life experiences, and enhanced intuitive awareness. Others report merely the feeling of a gentle warm glow enveloping their body.

In a new Reiki Practitioner, there are often energetic blocks, unhealthy beliefs, or patterns of behavior that need to be released through a cleansing process. The cleansing process begins during the attunement and typically lasts 21 days (3 days for each of the 7 major chakras) though each experience is unique to the individual.

This process may cause physical symptoms such as a headache, stomachache, or tiredness as toxins are cleared from the body. They may also experience temporary emotional or behavioral changes, such as increased joy or sadness, unexplained moodiness, changes in energy levels, or interesting dreams, as the unhealthy beliefs and negative patterns are released.

When preparing an client or student for an attunement, be sure to discuss the cleansing process with them so they are prepared to take care of themselves. Too many students come into a Reiki class without realizing that the class is only the beginning of their relationship with Reiki and there are things they will need to do after they leave class.

It is a good idea to recommend journaling to your students to help them maintain a high level of awareness during their cleansing experience. Be sure to emphasize the need to care for themselves during the cleansing process in whatever way they need, including seeking medical attention. They may need more rest and fluids, and often students report needing to accept changes to the way they eat (many students report not wanting to eat meat), or find ways to spend more time in quiet contemplation.

Every attunement and cleansing experience is unique to the individual, fine-tuned by spiritually guided energy to meet the needs of each new Reiki Practitioner. No experience is better than another, as each is uniquely crafted for the individual. Be careful not to let your or your students' expectations define what should be, or what a correct attunement experience looks and feels like. Trust that what is, is exactly what it should be.

Reiki Healing Attunements

Reiki Healing Attunements are unique in that they are the only type of attunement that DO NOT attune the participant to be able to work with Reiki energy. The purpose of a Reiki Healing Attunement is to provide a higher frequency of healing energy to either an individual or a group.

Reiki Healing Attunements can be helpful in creating clarity and increasing focus when someone is struggling with a specific issue, has an energy block around a goal they are trying to achieve, or if someone's energy feels a bit chaotic before a Reiki session. Where Reiki energy comes gently into our river of Life Force Energy to remove blockages, Reiki attunement energy can sometimes act as a flash flood, creating an easier path for both Reiki and Life Force Energy to flow.

As mentioned above, Reiki Healing Attunements can be given to an individual or a group, and are a great way to add Reiki to group gatherings you may already lead.

This book will share how to do a Reiki Healing Attunement with Dai Ko Myo for those who are completing the Level II/ART training only. Please note that once you are attuned to Holy Fire it will be added to the symbols used during the Healing Attunement.

Giving a Reiki Healing Attunement

The client should be sitting in a chair, with their feet flat on the ground, eyes closed, and their hands resting in their lap. Ensure you have enough space to walk completely around the chair and can stand both in back and in front of them comfortably.

Guide the client to focus inward and feel free to do a short breathing exercise or meditation to help them center. It is important to note that this practice is also a form of empowerment for your client, as it is them who must identify the block within and ultimately make the decision of whether or not to release what comes forward.

As you begin guiding the client to identify characteristics of the block, you may invite them to share out loud what they "see", however you may want to let them know that it isn't necessary and it is up to them to decide whether or not to share out loud. Remember that this is ultimately between them and Source, you are merely the intermediary and do not need to know what they are struggling with to help them find healing. In addition, without the pressure to share, people are given permission to explore areas they may not feel comfortable discussing, which allows them the space to process more deeply.

Healing Attunement Preparation Script

The script below is provided to assist you in preparing your client for a Reiki Healing Attunement to clear a specific block. Feel free to adjust the languaging to suit your style as needed.

"I invite you to allow your eyes to gently close, and I ask that they remain closed throughout the duration of the attunement. Let's start with a few centering breaths, just allowing your breath to expand more fully throughout your belly and your chest, and on the exhale allowing all that does not serve you to be released. We'll take 3 of these breaths, nice full breath in, full exhale, allowing the exhale to be longer than the inhale, and then one more, expanding the belly, the chest, and then letting them fall as you exhale it all away. Then I invite you to release any control of your breathing and return to the natural breath.

Now I will invite you to begin thinking about an issue you are currently struggling with. Allowing it to come fully into consciousness, but only as fully present as you feel comfortable with. If the emotions around it are too much right now, that's ok. If the physical sensations of it are not where you can comfortably go, that's ok too. Just allow the issue to come into your consciousness in a way that allows you to focus on that issue and that issue only. I invite you to allow everything else to fall away in this moment.

Now, if you know what the cause of the issue is, I invite you to allow your focus to shift to the cause. If you don't know, or maybe you aren't quite sure, than don't force it, just maintain your focus on the issue itself. We don't always need to know the cause for Source to help us heal, so don't worry too much about it.

(Skip this paragraph if leading a group) Next, I will invite you to consider the following questions, and whether you choose to answer them aloud is completely up to you. It won't impact the healing that takes place, so please do what you feel comfortable with.

If the issue, or the cause of the issue, was located somewhere in your body, where would it be? Maybe it's in your foot, your right bicep, near your navel… don't overthink it, just go with the first thought that comes to mind. (pause)

Once you have located the issue or cause of the issue in your body, take a few moments to imagine its characteristics.

What color is it? Maybe red, green, brown, or blue… Does it have a specific shape? Is it round, square, or maybe a pyramid… What size is it? Maybe it is small, like a grain of sand, or big like the size of a Volkswagen Bug. Does it have a temperature?... Does it move?... Make any sounds?... what else do you notice about it? (pause)

Now that you have located the issue or cause of the issue in your body, I invite you to focus on the image you have discovered, but do not become too attached to what you see. Remember to allow for changes to occur, including a full dissolution of the image. Ask yourself if you are really truly ready to let this go and then invite Source in to help clear it from your body. Please do your best to remain still, with your eyes closed, as I continue with the attunement process. Just relax and remember to stay open to any possible guidance that may come forward."

Dai Ko Myo Healing Attunement

<u>Preparation for the Healing Attunement</u>

As part of preparation for an attunement, it is recommended that you clear the room using the power symbol either before your client arrives, or once they are seated with their eyes closed.

Once you have finished preparing the client by focusing them on their issue or block, you must prepare yourself. Begin to flow Reiki, and ask for guidance in setting your ego aside, ask for any guides you would like to have join you, and set the intention for the Healing Attunement.

Next, while continuing to flow Reiki, draw Choku Rei over each of your seven major chakras, on both of your palm chakras, and over your entire body from crown to base chakra, remembering to push each symbol in three times.

Now you are ready to begin!

Dai Ko Myo Healing Attunement

Part One – Standing Behind Your Client

1. Creating Energetic Resonance

This is an important first step, and the initial contact between you and your client, as well as the initial introduction to Reiki energy. While flowing Reiki, place your hands gently on their shoulders and allow a moment to feel an energetic resonance build between you. Then re-affirm the intention for the Healing Attunement by stating it using your inner voice.

2. Placing the Symbols

Hold your non-dominant hand slightly above and to the side of the client's head. Then using your dominant hand begin to draw the Master symbol, Dai Ko Myo, over the crown. Then saying the name of the symbol to yourself as you do, direct it into to crown of the head, the center of the back of the head, and finally into the back of the heart. Repeat this step with Choku Rei, Sei Heki, and Hon Sha Ze Sho Nen.

Dai Ko Myo Healing Attunement

Part Two – Standing in Front of Your Client

1. Placing the Symbols

Facing your client, hold your non-dominant hand slightly above and to the side of the client's head. With your dominant hand begin to draw the Master symbol, Dai Ko Myo, over the Crown Chakra. Then saying the name of the symbol to yourself as you do, direct it into the Third Eye Chakra, the Heart Chakra, and finally into the Solar Plexus Chakra. Repeat this step with Choku Rei, Sei Heki, and Hon Sha Ze Sho Nen.

2. Moving the Breath

This is done in one LONG continuous breath, with your hands moving in the direction of your breath. Begin with your hands about 12-18 inches (20-30cm) in front of the client, with your fingers together and pointed at the client's Base Chakra, palms facing upwards, almost as if you are offering something to them. (cont. on next page)

Dai Ko Myo Healing Attunement

(Moving the Breath cont) …

Begin to blow gently into their Base Chakra, moving up along the Sacral Chakra, Solar Plexus Chakra, the Heart Chakra, Throat Chakra, Third Eye Chakra, and the Crown Chakra, then turning palms facing down, continue blowing back down the body all the way to the Base Chakra, then turn palms upwards again, and push up past the Crown Chakra as you push out the last of your breath. As you are moving your hands you are guiding the energy, with the final push up and out designed to remove any negative energy that might have been present, so feel free to give the breath a little force.

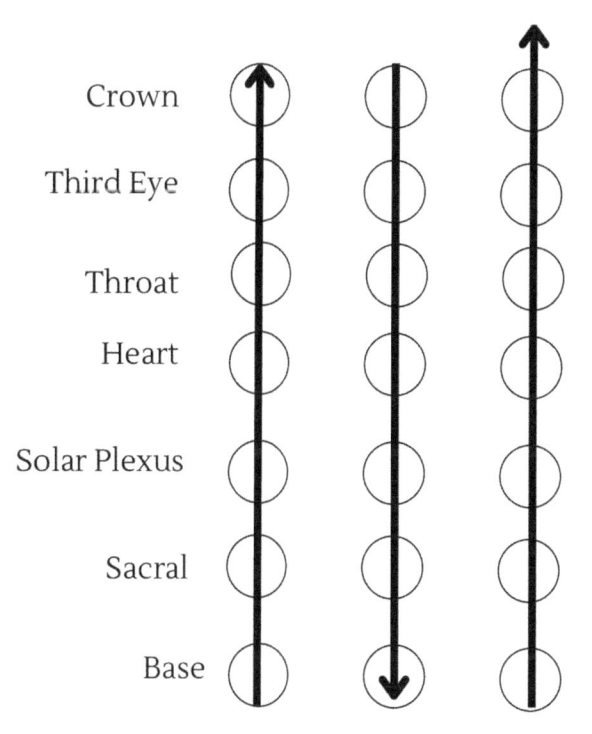

Dai Ko Myo Healing Attunement

Part three – Standing Behind Your Client

1. Sharing an Affirmation

Gently place your hands on the client's shoulders. Using your mind's eye, look down through the Client's Crown Chakra, imagining that you can see into their Heart Space. Imagine that you see a ball of light in their heart space and share an affirmation to be held in that Heart Space with the beautiful light.

There are many options for an affirmation, feel free to choose one that works for you, but here are a few options to get you started:

- "You are healed with Divine Love"
- "You are loved and cared for by the Divine"
- "You have all you need to heal within you"
- "You are empowered in your healing by Divine Love".

Dai Ko Myo Healing Attunement

2. Sealing the Attunement

Place your dominant hand on the back of the client's Heart Chakra, leaving your non-dominant hand on their shoulder. Imagine a Choku Rei symbol on the back of the Heart Chakra, and with the intention to complete and seal the attunement repeat the following phrase to yourself three times, "I seal this Healing Attunement with Love & Light".

3. Blessings & Gratitude

Place both hands upon the client's shoulders once again and take a moment to share gratitude for the blessings that have taken place here today, both for the client and yourself.

Dai Ko Myo Healing Attunement

<u>Part Four – Standing in Front of Your Client</u>

1. Gratitude to your Client

Standing a few feet in front of your client, bring your hands to the Gassho prayer position and give gratitude to your client for allowing you to be part of their healing journey. Then turn your fingers inwards, towards your Heart Chakra with the backs of your hands facing each other, sweep your hands out wide to the sides of your body and bow to your client as a show of gratitude and respect.

2. Optional: Check in on presence of "block"

Ask your client to keep their eyes closed, but to take a few centering breaths and then check in on the location of their identified block or issue. Ask if they notice any changes to the size of it, or if perhaps it is gone completely. If it remains, then additional healing is needed, if it is gone, then the issue has been healed. Either way, you may continue with a standard Reiki session.

Dai Ko Myo Healing Attunement Quick Guide

Part One – Behind Your Client

1. Resonance: hands on shoulders, set intention
2. Symbols: draw above crown, motion into crown, back of head, and heart

Part Two – In Front of Your Client

1. Symbols: draw above crown, motion into third eye, heart, solar plexus
2. Moving the Breath: start at Base Chakra, up to Crown, Back down to the Base, and back up and out past the Crown!

Part three – Behind Your Client

1. Affirmation: hands on shoulders, top of head to heart, set affirmation
2. Sealing: hand and Choku Rei on back of heart space
3. Blessings: hands on shoulders, give gratitude

Part Four – In Front of Your Client

1. Gratitude to your Client: hands together, open in bow
Optional: Check in on presence of "block"

Create Your Own Dai Ko Myo Healing Attunement Quick Guide

Chapter 3

Usui Holy Fire Reiki Master

Becoming a Reiki Master

Becoming a Reiki Master is about deepening your relationship with Reiki, with Spiritual Consciousness. The changes you experienced during your Level I and Level II attunements were merely preparing you for what's to come. At the level of Reiki Master, it becomes clear that Reiki is more than just a thing you do, it's a way of life. Through the Holy Fire ignition process, you are given the opportunity to more fully embody Reiki energy, connecting to the essence of Spiritual Consciousness, and moving into the life of a Reiki Master.

So, what is the Reiki Master Life? Well, that is up to you and Spiritual Consciousness. The relationship you create with Reiki is as unique as you are. Just as working with Level I and II energy helped connect you more deeply to your spiritual gifts and becoming attuned to Dai Ko Myo helped you connect with your Inner Reiki Master, becoming a Usui Holy Fire Reiki Master connects you more directly to Spiritual Consciousness, giving you the potential to attune new Reiki Practitioners, further sharing the love of Reiki with the world. Whether you decide to teach or not, your raised frequency will have an impact wherever you go in the world, and what you decide to do with that is up to you.

Usui Holy Fire Reiki

Usui Holy Fire is a specific type of Reiki energy that was channeled by William Rand of the ICRT and shared as a practice for the first time in January of 2014. The biggest difference between Usui Holy Fire Reiki and Usui Reiki is the initiation of a more direct connection between Spiritual Consciousness and the Reiki Master Student. There is less ritual involved on the part of the initiating Reiki Master, their primary role becoming more about holding space than being a conduit for the Reiki energy.

Dr. Campbell was fortunate to be a part of the initial Holy Fire Reiki class at William's home on the island of Maui, below is her story.

"In January of 2014 I flew to Hawaii to attend Usui Reiki Master Training with William Rand of the ICRT. The first day of class, there were about 10 of us gathered as William explained he had been working on connecting to a new type of Reiki energy and that instead of what we had been expecting to learn and be attuned to, we would be working with this new energy instead. We were all pretty surprised, and quite a few of us were unsure about it (including me), but after discussing it as a group and asking William some questions, we all agreed to move forward and see where things went.

As it was William's first time working with Reiki in this way, there were no class manuals, so we used the ICRT's Usui Reiki Master manuals and just made notes and crossed things out as we went along. It felt a bit like a group project at times, as we all began to connect with the Holy Fire energy and share our experiences; how it felt when we did something one way vs. another, and what the symbol looked and felt like to each of us.

The way the Holy Fire symbol presented to us felt very different from the other Reiki symbols, as it felt very much alive. When we drew the flame of Holy Fire on our palms we could see and feel it move and change shape like an actual flame.

The other thing that made working with Holy Fire Reiki so different is that William was guided not to do standard attunements with this new energy. He shared that with Holy Fire Reiki he was guided not to perform any ritual, but instead just hold space. Trusting his guidance, William led us to line up a row of chairs outside, guided us very briefly using a short meditation, and then sat in front of us holding space. At the end of about 20 minutes, he told us the process was complete and for each of us to take our own time coming back from the experience. As soon as William was back in the house, I heard wind coming from my right. At the sound we all began to open our eyes and saw a wind tunnel heading towards us from the field nearby. It came so quickly we had no time to react as we watched it go straight to the chair William had been sitting in, raising the chair high up into the air and then carrying it about 50 yards where it dissipated and dropped the chair. To say we were stunned would be an understatement… I was completely in shock. We all just sat there silently for a few minutes as we tried to make sense of what we saw. Eventually we began to chat and make our way up to the house, only to find out William had missed the whole thing! A few of the others said they believed it was the Holy Spirt, and one of the students said it was the answer to her prayer asking for a sign about the new Reiki energy. For me it just reinforced that this new energy was about our own personal connections with Holy Fire Reiki versus having to be guided through the ritual of attunement by a Reiki Master.

By the end of our three-day class I was convinced that Spirit had once again led me to exactly where I needed to be. Though we still practice attunements for Usui Holy Fire Reiki I, II, and III, at the level of Reiki Master there is a deeply personal relationship being created between the student and Spiritual Consciousness, it's about so much more than simply being attuned to a higher frequency. During these moments I am just grateful to be a guide, holding space and intention as the connection is created."

Dr. Adrian Campbell

Holy Fire

Reiki Level I, II, III/ART Attunements

The previous chapter discussed the basics of the attunement process, which is foundationally the same for all attunements. For each style of attunement you prepare yourself and the room in the same way, the differences begin with your stated intention and how the symbols are used, more specifically, which are put into the hands of the student, and which are not. The Healing Attunement is the only attunement where NONE of the symbols are put into the hands of the client, as that attunement is not intended to allow them to begin practicing Reiki.

The following sections include detailed instructions for each type of attunement, as well as a Quick Guide. At the end of each section there is space for you to create your own Quick Guide, and it is highly recommended that you use that space to create instructions using language and images familiar to you for reference while you are practicing your attunements.

Be sure to take your time with the process, remembering that this isn't just about following written steps, but as a Reiki Master you are holding space for a very special event and performing an important ritual to help connect this individual with Spiritual Consciousness. Though it may feel a bit clunky in the beginning as you learn, once you have the mechanics of it down it is important to return to the sacredness of the moment.

> As a reminder, this book shares how to do Reiki attunements using the Holy Fire symbol. If you are not trained as a Usui Holy Fire Reiki Master the process you were taught will be different. Please note that to use the Holy Fire symbol you must go through the Usui Holy Fire Reiki Master guided ignition process as outlined later in this book.

Giving Attunements to Groups vs. Individuals

Most often Reiki attunements are given to a group of students as part of a class or healing event, but they can also be given individually during one-on-one trainings, or as a booster attunement to someone already attuned to a certain level.

To give an attunement to multiple students, place them in chairs lined up in a row or in a circle, ensuring that you have space to move behind and in front of them. Complete each part of the attunement process for each of your students, before moving on to the next one. For example, Part One of each attunement has multiple steps, which include creating rapport, setting the intention, and placing symbols from behind the student. For a group, you would do every step of this Part of the attunement for each student. Once the steps for that Part of the attunement are complete, you would move from the back of one student to the next, until that step was complete for all individuals in the group. Next, for Part Two, you would move to the front of the students and begin going down the row of chairs completing each step of Part Two for each student, until that Part was complete, and so on for each remaining Part of the attunement process, ending with the final step of a bow to each student.

Usui Holy Fire Reiki Healing Attunement

<u>Preparation for the Healing Attunement</u>

As part of preparation for an attunement, it is recommended that you clear the room using the Holy Fire symbol either before your client arrives, or once they are seated with their eyes closed.

Once you have finished preparing the client by focusing them on their issue or block, you must prepare yourself. Begin to flow Reiki, and ask for guidance in setting your ego aside, ask for any guides you would like to have join you, and set the intention for the Healing Attunement.

Next, while continuing to flow Reiki, draw the Holy Fire symbol over each of your seven major chakras, on both of your palm chakras, and over your entire body from crown to base chakra, remembering to push each symbol in three times.

Now you are ready to begin!

Usui Holy Fire Reiki Healing Attunement

Part One – Standing Behind Your Client

1. Creating Energetic Resonance

This is an important first step, and the initial contact between you and your client, as well as the initial introduction to Reiki energy. While flowing Reiki, place your hands gently on their shoulders and allow a moment to feel an energetic resonance build between you. Then re-affirm the intention for the Healing Attunement by stating it using your inner voice.

2. Placing the Symbols

Hold your non-dominant hand slightly above and to the side of the client's head. Then using your dominant hand begin to draw the Holy Fire over the crown. Then saying the name of the symbol to yourself as you do, direct it into to crown of the head, the center of the back of the head, and finally into the back of the heart. Repeat this step with Dai Ko Myo, Choku Rei, Sei Heki, and Hon Sha Ze Sho Nen.

Usui Holy Fire Reiki Healing Attunement

<u>Part Two – Standing in Front of Your Client</u>

1. Placing the Symbols

Facing your client, hold your non-dominant hand slightly above and to the side of the client's head. With your dominant hand begin to draw Holy Fire over the Crown Chakra. Then saying the name of the symbol to yourself as you do, direct it into the Third Eye Chakra, the Heart Chakra, and finally into the Solar Plexus Chakra. Repeat this step with Dai Ko Myo, Choku Rei, Sei Heki, and Hon Sha Ze Sho Nen.

2. Moving the Breath

This is done in one LONG continuous breath, with your hands moving in the direction of your breath. Begin with your hands about 12-18 inches (20-30cm) in front of the client, with your fingers together and pointed at the client's Base Chakra, palms facing upwards, almost as if you are offering something to them. (cont. on next page)

Usui Holy Fire Reiki Healing Attunement

(Moving the Breath cont) ...

Begin to blow gently into their Base Chakra, moving up along the Sacral Chakra, Solar Plexus Chakra, the Heart Chakra, Throat Chakra, Third Eye Chakra, and the Crown Chakra, then turning palms facing down, continue blowing back down the body all the way to the Base Chakra, then turn palms upwards again, and push up past the Crown Chakra as you push out the last of your breath. As you are moving your hands you are guiding the energy, with the final push up and out designed to remove any negative energy that might have been present, so feel free to give the breath a little force.

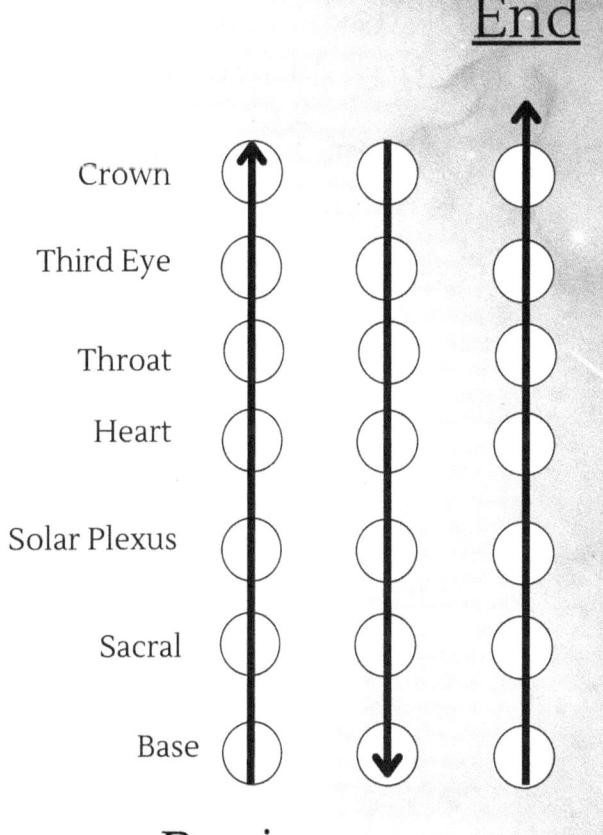

Usui Holy Fire Reiki Healing Attunement

<u>Part three – Standing Behind Your Client</u>

1. Sharing an Affirmation

Gently place your hands on the client's shoulders. Using your mind's eye, look down through the Client's Crown Chakra, imagining that you can see into their Heart Space. Imagine that you see a ball of light in their heart space and share an affirmation to be held in that Heart Space with the beautiful light.

There are many options for an affirmation, feel free to choose one that works for you, but here are a few options to get you started:

- "You are healed with Divine Love"
- "You are loved and cared for by the Divine"
- "You have all you need to heal within you"
- "You are empowered in your healing by Divine Love".

Usui Holy Fire Reiki Healing Attunement

2. Sealing the Attunement

Place your dominant hand on the back of the client's Heart Chakra, leaving your non-dominant hand on their shoulder. Imagine a Choku Rei symbol on the back of the Heart Chakra, and with the intention to complete and seal the attunement repeat the following phrase to yourself three times, "I seal this Healing Attunement with Love & Light".

3. Blessings & Gratitude

Place both hands upon the client's shoulders once again and take a moment to share gratitude for the blessings that have taken place here today, both for the client and yourself.

Usui Holy Fire Reiki Healing Attunement

Part Four – Standing in Front of Your Client

1. Gratitude to your Client

Standing a few feet in front of your client, bring your hands to the Gassho prayer position and give gratitude to your client for allowing you to be part of their healing journey. Then turn your fingers inwards, towards your Heart Chakra with the backs of your hands facing each other, sweep your hands out wide to the sides of your body and bow to your client as a show of gratitude and respect.

2. Optional: Check in on presence of "block"

Ask your client to keep their eyes closed, but to take a few centering breaths and then check in on the location of their identified block or issue. Ask if they notice any changes to the size of it, or if perhaps it is gone completely. If it remains, then additional healing is needed, and if it is gone, then the issue has been healed. Either way, you may continue with a standard Reiki session.

Usui Holy Fire Reiki Healing Attunement Quick Guide

Part One – Behind Your Client

1. Resonance: hands on shoulders, set intention
2. Symbols: draw above crown, motion into crown, back of head, and heart

Part Two – In Front of Your Client

1. Symbols: draw above crown, motion into third eye, heart, solar plexus
2. Moving the Breath: start at Base Chakra, up to Crown, Back down to the Base, and back up and out past the Crown!

Part three – Behind Your Client

1. Affirmation: hands on shoulders, top of head to heart, set affirmation
2. Sealing: hand and Choku Rei on back of heart space
3. Blessings: hands on shoulders, give gratitude

Part Four – In Front of Your Client

1. Gratitude to your Client: hands together, open in bow
Optional: Check in on presence of "block"

Create Your Own Usui Holy Fire Reiki Healing Attunement Quick Guide

Usui Holy Fire Reiki Level I Attunement

Preparation for the Attunement

As part of preparation for an attunement, it is recommended that you clear the room using the Holy Fire symbol, either before your student arrives, or once they are seated with their eyes closed.

For a Reiki Level 1 Attunement, the student should be sitting in a chair, with their feet flat on the ground, eyes closed, and their hands Gassho prayer position. Ensure you have enough space to walk completely around the chair and be able to stand both in back and in front of them comfortably.

Guide the student to focus inward and feel free to do a short breathing exercise or meditation to help them center. To prepare yourself, begin to flow Reiki. Ask for guidance in setting your ego aside, for any guides you would like to have join you, and set the intention for a Reiki Level 1 Attunement.

Next, while continuing to flow Reiki, draw Holy Fire over each of your seven major chakras, on both of your palm chakras, and over your entire body from crown to base chakra, remembering to push each symbol in three times.

Usui Holy Fire Reiki Level I Attunement

Part One – Standing Behind Your Client

1. Creating Energetic Resonance

This is an important first step, and the initial contact between you and your student, as well as the initial introduction to Reiki energy. While flowing Reiki, place your hands gently on their shoulders and allow a moment to feel an energetic resonance build between you. Then re-affirm the intention for a Reiki Level 1 Attunement by stating it using your inner voice.

2. Placing the Symbols

Hold your non-dominant hand slightly above and to the side of the student's head. Then using your dominant hand begin to draw the Holy Fire over the crown. Then saying the name of the symbol to yourself as you do, direct it into to crown of the head, the center of the back of the head, and finally into the base of the skull. Repeat this step with Dai Ko Myo, Sei Heki, and Hon Sha Ze Sho Nen. (Note: you are intentionally skipping Choku Rei).

Usui Holy Fire
Reiki Level I Attunement

3. Hands above head

Reach over the student and bring their hands up to rest on top of their head. Help them maintain prayer position by using your non-dominant hand to hold theirs together.

4. Symbol into Hands

Continue holding the student's hands with your non-dominant hand, while you use your dominant hand to draw Choku Rei above the student's fingertips, and then direct the symbol into the hands and crown of the head, the center of the back of the head, and finally into the base of the skull, repeating Choku Rei to yourself as you do.

5. Return their Hands

Gently guide your student's hands back down towards the center of their chest

Usui Holy Fire Reiki Level I Attunement

Part Two – Standing in Front of Your Client

1. Placing the Symbols

Facing your student, gently bring their hands down into their lap, opening them, palms facing up to rest on your non-dominant hand. Using your dominant hand, draw Choku Rei above one palm, then tap it into the hand three times, repeating the name of the symbol to yourself as you do. Repeat these steps for the remaining palm, and then return the student's hands back to prayer position in front of their Heart Chakra

2. Moving the Breath

This is done in one LONG continuous breath, with your hands moving in the direction of your breath. As you are moving your hands you are guiding the energy between the chakras and then into the hands and heart (cont. on next page)

Usui Holy Fire
Reiki Level I Attunement

(Moving the Breath cont) ...

Begin with your hands about 12-18 inches (20-30cm) in front of the client, with your fingers together and pointed at the student's Heart Chakra begin to blow gently into their Heart Chakra, turning palms down, move your breath down to the Solar Plexus Chakra, turn palms up and move your breath along the chakras, up to the Crown Chakra, and then once again turning palms facing down, continue blowing back down the body to the Solar Plexus Chakra, then turn palms upwards again, to push out the last of your breath into the hands at the Heart Chakra.

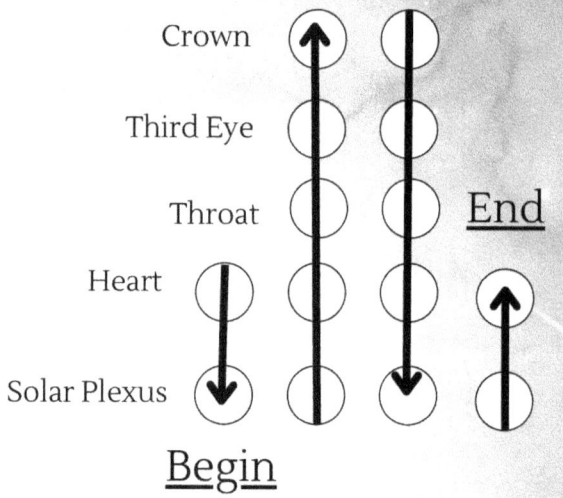

Usui Holy Fire
Reiki Level I Attunement

<u>Part three – Standing Behind Your Client</u>

1. Sharing an Affirmation

Gently place your hands on the student's shoulders. Using your mind's eye, look down through the Student's Crown Chakra, imagining that you can see all the way down into their Root Chakra. Imagine that you see a ball of red light representative of their Root Chakra and share an affirmation to be held in that space with the beautiful light.

There are many options for an affirmation, feel free to choose one that works for you, but here are a few options to get you started:

- "You are now a powerful Level I Reiki Practitioner"
- "You are a powerful and successful Reiki Level I Practitioner"
- "You are now a Reiki Level I Practitioner guided by divine love & wisdom"

Usui Holy Fire Reiki Level I Attunement

2. Sealing the Attunement

Tuck your fingers into your palms in gentle fists, with your thumbs held loosely on top, place your thumbs on either side of the base of the student's skull, and with the intention to complete and seal the attunement, repeat the following phrase to yourself three times, "I seal this Reiki Level I Attunement with Love & Light".

3. Blessings & Gratitude

Place both hands upon the student's shoulders once again and take a moment to share gratitude for the blessings that have taken place here today, both for the student and yourself.

Usui Holy Fire Reiki Level I Attunement

<u>Part Four – Standing in Front of Your Student</u>

1. Gratitude to your Student

Standing a few feet in front of your student, bring your hands to the Gassho prayer position and give gratitude to your student for allowing you to be part of their healing journey. Then turn your fingers inwards, towards your Heart Chakra with the backs of your hands facing each other, sweep your hands out wide to the sides of your body and bow to your student as a show of gratitude and respect.

2. Bringing them Back to Awareness

State out loud "the attunement process is now complete", and guide your student to begin to feel into their body, supported and grounded in their chair, to take a few centering breaths, and when they are ready, to open their eyes and spend a few moments in reflection and journaling about their experience.

Usui Holy Fire Reiki Level I Attunement Quick Guide

Part One – Behind Your Student

1. Resonance: hands on shoulders, set intention
2. Symbols: draw Holy Fire, Dai Ko Myo, Sei Heki, and Hon Sha Ze Sho Nen above crown, motion into crown, back of head, and base of skull (skip Choku Rei)
3. Hands Above Head: Choku Rei above hands and into crown, back of head, and base of skull

Part Two – In Front of Your Student

1. Symbols: open the hands, draw Choku Rei and tap into palms 3x
2. Moving the Breath: start at Heart, down to Solar Plexus, up to Third Eye, Crown, down to Solar Plexus, and back up and into hands!

Part three – Behind Your Student

1. Affirmation: hands on shoulders, top of head to Base Chakra, set affirmation
2. Sealing: thumbs at base of skull
3. Blessings: hands on shoulders, give gratitude

Part Four – In Front of Your Student

1. Gratitude to Student: hands together, open in bow

Create Your Own Usui Holy Fire Reiki Level I Attunement Quick Guide

Usui Holy Fire
Reiki Level II Attunement

Preparation for the Attunement

As part of preparation for an attunement, it is recommended that you clear the room using the Holy Fire symbol, either before your student arrives, or once they are seated with their eyes closed.

For a Reiki Level II Attunement, the student should be sitting in a chair, with their feet flat on the ground, eyes closed, and their hands Gassho prayer position. Ensure you have enough space to walk completely around the chair and be able to stand both in back and in front of them comfortably.

Guide the student to focus inward and feel free to do a short breathing exercise or meditation to help them center. To prepare yourself, begin to flow Reiki. Ask for guidance in setting your ego aside, for any guides you would like to have join you, and set the intention for a Reiki Level II Attunement.

Next, while continuing to flow Reiki, draw Holy Fire over each of your seven major chakras, on both of your palm chakras, and over your entire body from crown to base chakra, remembering to push each symbol in three times.

Usui Holy Fire
Reiki Level II Attunement

Part One – Standing Behind Your Student

1. Creating Energetic Resonance

This is an important first step, and the initial contact between you and your student, as well as the initial introduction to Reiki energy. While flowing Reiki, place your hands gently on their shoulders and allow a moment to feel an energetic resonance build between you. Then re-affirm the intention for a Reiki Level II Attunement by stating it using your inner voice.

2. Placing the Symbols

Holding your non-dominant hand slightly above and to the side of the student's head, then using your dominant hand begin to draw the Holy Fire symbol, over the crown, saying the name of the symbol to yourself as you do, direct it into to crown of the head, the center of the back of the head, and finally into the base of the skull. Repeat this step with Dai Ko Myo (Note: you are intentionally skipping Choku Rei, Sei Heki, and Hon Sha Ze Sho Nen).

Usui Holy Fire
Reiki Level II Attunement

3. Hands above head

Reach over the student and bring their hands up to rest on top of their head. Help them maintain prayer position by using your non-dominant hand to hold theirs together.

4. Symbols into Hands

Continue holding the student's hands with your non-dominant hand, while you use your dominant hand to draw Choku Rei above the student's fingertips, and then direct the symbol into the hands and crown of the head, the center of the back of the head, and finally into the base of the skull, repeating Choku Rei to yourself as you do. Repeat this step with Sei Heki and Hon Sha Ze Sho Nen.

5. Return their Hands

Gently guide your student's hands back down towards the center of their chest.

Usui Holy Fire
Reiki Level II Attunement

<u>Part Two – Standing in Front of Your Client</u>

1. Placing the Symbols

Facing your student, gently bring their hands down into their lap, opening them, palms facing up to rest on your non-dominant hand. Using your dominant hand, draw Choku Rei above one palm, then tap it into the hand three times, repeating the name of the symbol to yourself as you do. Follow the same steps for the remaining palm, and then repeat the entire sequence for Sei Heki and Hon Sha Ze Sho Nen. Once you are finished, return the student's hands back to prayer position in front of their Heart Chakra

2. Moving the Breath

This is done in one LONG continuous breath, with your hands moving in the direction of your breath. As you are moving your hands you are guiding the energy between the chakras and then into the hands and heart (cont. on next page)

Usui Holy Fire
Reiki Level II Attunement

(Moving the Breath cont)…

Begin with your hands about 12-18 inches (20-30cm) in front of the client, with your fingers together and pointed at the student's Heart Chakra. Begin to blow gently into their Heart Chakra, turning palms down, move your breath down to the Solar Plexus Chakra, turn palms up and move your breath along the chakras, up to the Crown Chakra, and then once again turning palms facing down, continue blowing back down the body to the Solar Plexus Chakra, then turn palms upwards again, to push out the last of your breath into the hands at the Heart Chakra.

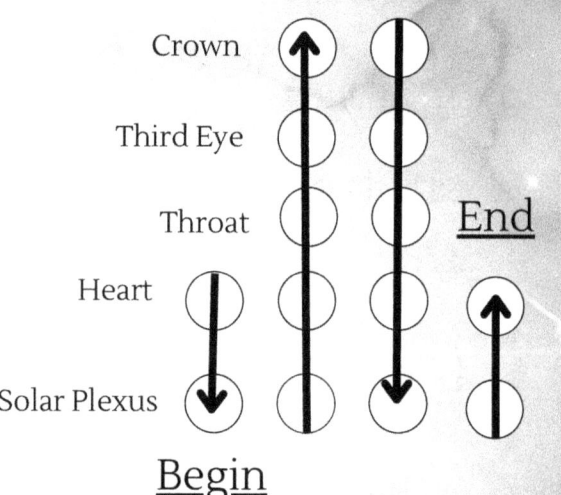

Usui Holy Fire Reiki Level II Attunement

Part three – Standing Behind Your Student

1. Sharing an Affirmation

Gently place your hands on the student's shoulders. Using your mind's eye, look down through the Student's Crown Chakra, imagining that you can see all the way down into their Root Chakra. Imagine that you see a ball of red light representative of their Root Chakra and share an affirmation to be held in that space with the beautiful light.

There are many options for an affirmation, feel free to choose one that works for you, but here are a few options to get you started:

- "You are now a powerful Level II Reiki Practitioner"
- "You are a powerful and successful Reiki Level II Practitioner"
- "You are now a Reiki Level II Practitioner guided by divine love & wisdom"

Usui Holy Fire
Reiki Level II Attunement

2. Sealing the Attunement

Tuck your fingers into your palms in gentle fists, with your thumbs held loosely on top, place your thumbs on either side of the base of the student's skull, and with the intention to complete and seal the attunement, repeat the following phrase to yourself three times, "I seal this Reiki Level II Attunement with Love & Light".

3. Blessings & Gratitude

Place both hands upon the student's shoulders once again and take a moment to share gratitude for the blessings that have taken place here today, both for the student and yourself.

Usui Holy Fire Reiki Level II Attunement

Part Four – Standing in Front of Your Student

1. Gratitude to Your Student

Standing a few feet in front of your student, bring your hands to the Gassho prayer position and give gratitude to your student for allowing you to be part of their healing journey. Then turn your fingers inwards, towards your Heart Chakra with the backs of your hands facing each other, sweep your hands out wide to the sides of your body and bow to your student as a show of gratitude and respect.

2. Bringing them Back to Awareness

State out loud "the attunement process is now complete", and guide your student to begin to feel into their body, supported and grounded in their chair, to take a few centering breaths, and when they are ready, to open their eyes and spend a few moments in reflection and journaling about their experience.

Usui Holy Fire Reiki Level II Attunement Quick Guide

Part One – Behind Your Student

1. Resonance: draw Holy Fire and Dai Ko Myo above crown, motion into crown, back of head, and base of skull (skip Choku Rei, Sei Heki, and Hon Sha Ze Sho Nen)
3. Hands Above Head: Choku Rei, Sei Heki, and Hon Sha Ze Sho Nen above hands and into crown, back of head, and base of skull

Part Two – In Front of Your Student

1. Symbols: open the hands, draw Choku Rei, Sei Heki, and Hon Sha Ze Sho Nen and tap into palms 3x
2. Moving the Breath: start at Heart, down to Solar Plexus, up to Third Eye, Crown, down to Solar Plexus, and back up and into hands!

Part three – Behind Your Student

1. Affirmation: hands on shoulders, top of head to Base Chakra, set affirmation
2. Sealing: thumbs at base of skull
3. Blessings: hands on shoulders, give gratitude

Part Four – In Front of Your Student

1. Gratitude to Student: hands together, open in bow

Create Your Own Usui Holy Fire Reiki Level II Attunement Quick Guide

Usui Holy Fire
Reiki Level III/ART Attunement

<u>Preparation for the Attunement</u>

As part of preparation for an attunement, it is recommended that you clear the room using the Holy Fire symbol, either before your student arrives, or once they are seated with their eyes closed.

For a Reiki Level II Attunement, the student should be sitting in a chair, with their feet flat on the ground, eyes closed, and their hands Gassho prayer position. Ensure you have enough space to walk completely around the chair and be able to stand both in back and in front of them comfortably.

Guide the student to focus inward and feel free to do a short breathing exercise or meditation to help them center. To prepare yourself, begin to flow Reiki. Ask for guidance in setting your ego aside, for any guides you would like to have join you, and set the intention for a Reiki Level III/ART Attunement.

Next, while continuing to flow Reiki, draw Holy Fire over each of your seven major chakras, on both of your palm chakras, and over your entire body from crown to base chakra, remembering to push each symbol in three times.

Usui Holy Fire
Reiki Level III/ART Attunement

Part One – Standing Behind Your Student

1. Creating Energetic Resonance

This is an important first step, and the initial contact between you and your student, as well as the initial introduction to Reiki energy. While flowing Reiki, place your hands gently on their shoulders and allow a moment to feel an energetic resonance build between you. Then re-affirm the intention for a Reiki Level III/ART Attunement by stating it using your inner voice.

2. Placing the Symbols

Holding your non-dominant hand slightly above and to the side of the student's head, then using your dominant hand begin to draw the Holy Fire symbol, over the crown, saying the name of the symbol to yourself as you do, direct it into to crown of the head, the center of the back of the head, and finally into the base of the skull. (Note: you are intentionally skipping all of the other symbols).

Usui Holy Fire Reiki Level III/ART Attunement

3. Hands above head

Reach over the student and bring their hands up to rest on top of their head. Help them maintain prayer position by using your non-dominant hand to hold theirs together.

4. Symbol into Hands

Continue holding the student's hands with your non-dominant hand, while you use your dominant hand to draw Dai Ko Myo above the student's fingertips, and then direct the symbol into the hands and crown of the head, the center of the back of the head, and finally into the base of the skull, repeating Dai Ko Myo to yourself as you do. Repeat for Choku Rei, Sei Heki, and Hon Sha Ze Sho Nen.

5. Return their Hands

Gently guide your student's hands back down towards the center of their chest.

Usui Holy Fire Reiki Level III/ART Attunement

<u>Part Two – Standing in Front of Your Student</u>

1. Placing the Symbols

Facing your student, gently bring their hands down into their lap, opening them, palms facing up to rest on your non-dominant hand. Using your dominant hand, draw Dai Ko Myo above one palm, then tap it into the hand three times, repeating the name of the symbol to yourself as you do. Follow the same steps for the remaining palm, and then repeat the entire sequence for Choku Rei, Sei Heki, and Hon Sha Ze Sho Nen.

2. Moving the Breath

This is done in one LONG continuous breath, with your hands moving in the direction of your breath. As you are moving your hands you are guiding the energy between the chakras and then into the hands and heart (cont. on next page)

Usui Holy Fire Reiki Level III/ART Attunement

(Moving the Breath cont) …

Begin with your hands about 12-18 inches (20-30cm) in front of the client, with your fingers together and pointed at the student's Heart Chakra. Begin to blow gently into their Heart Chakra, turning palms down, move your breath down to the Solar Plexus Chakra, turn palms up and move your breath along the chakras, up to the Crown Chakra, and then once again turning palms facing down, continue blowing back down the body to the Solar Plexus Chakra, then turn palms upwards again, to push out the last of your breath into the hands at the Heart Chakra.

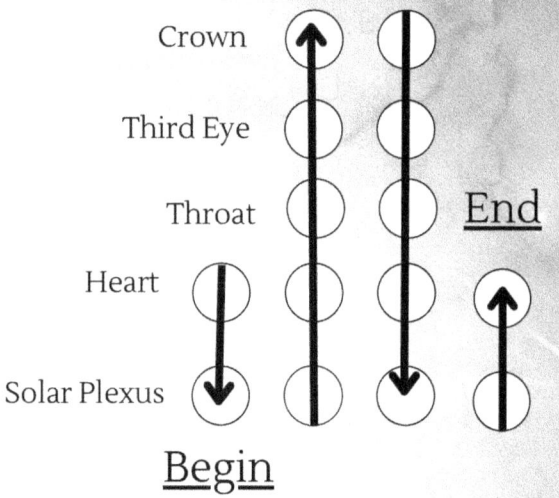

Usui Holy Fire
Reiki Level III/ART Attunement

Part three – Standing Behind Your Student

1. Sharing an Affirmation

Gently place your hands on the student's shoulders. Using your mind's eye, look down through the Student's Crown Chakra, imagining that you can see all the way down into their Root Chakra. Imagine that you see a ball of red light representative of their Root Chakra and share an affirmation to be held in that space with the beautiful light.

There are many options for an affirmation, feel free to choose one that works for you, but here are a few options to get you started:

- "You are now a powerful Level III Reiki Practitioner"
- "You are a powerful and successful Advanced Reiki Practitioner"
- "You are now an Advanced Reiki Level III Practitioner guided by divine love & wisdom".

Usui Holy Fire
Reiki Level III/ART Attunement

2. Sealing the Attunement

Tuck your fingers into your palms in gentle fists, with your thumbs held loosely on top, place your thumbs on either side of the base of the student's skull, and with the intention to complete and seal the attunement, repeat the following phrase to yourself three times, "I seal this Reiki Level III/ART Attunement with Love & Light".

3. Blessings & Gratitude

Place both hands upon the student's shoulders once again and take a moment to share gratitude for the blessings that have taken place here today, both for the student and yourself.

Usui Holy Fire Reiki Level III/ART Attunement

<u>Part Four – Standing in Front of Your Student</u>

1. Gratitude to your Student

Standing a few feet in front of your student, bring your hands to the Gassho prayer position and give gratitude to your client for allowing you to be part of their healing journey. Then turn your fingers inwards, towards your Heart Chakra with the backs of your hands facing each other, sweep your hands out wide to the sides of your body and bow to your student as a show of gratitude and respect.

2. Bringing them Back to Awareness

State out loud "the attunement process is now complete", and guide your students to begin to feel into their bodies, supported and grounded in their chairs, to take a few centering breaths, and when they are ready, to open their eyes and spend a few moments in reflection and journaling about their experience.

Usui Holy Fire Reiki Level III/ART Attunement Quick Guide

Part One – Behind Your Student

1. Resonance: draw Holy Fire above crown, motion into crown, back of head, and base of skull (skip all others)
3. Hands Above Head: Dai Ko Myo, Choku Rei, Sei Heki, and Hon Sha Ze Sho Nen above hands and into crown, back of head, and base of skull

Part Two – In Front of Your Student

1. Symbols: open the hands, draw Dai Ko Myo, Choku Rei, Sei Heki, and Hon Sha Ze Sho Nen and tap into palms 3x
2. Moving the Breath: start at Heart, down to Solar Plexus, up to Third Eye, Crown, down to Solar Plexus, and back up and into hands!

Part three – Behind Your Student

1. Affirmation: hands on shoulders, top of head to Base Chakra, set affirmation
2. Sealing: thumbs at base of skull
3. Blessings: hands on shoulders, give gratitude

Part Four – In Front of Your Student

1. Gratitude to Student: hands together, open in bow

Create Your Own Usui Holy Fire Reiki Level III/ART Attunement Quick Guide

Usui Holy Fire Reiki Master Ignitions

As mentioned earlier, there are no attunements for Usui Holy Fire Reiki Master, instead you will guide your students through what are called Ignitions. This process in comparison to the attunement process is literally hands-off, allowing the students to connect and commune with Spiritual Consciousness more independently of the Reiki Master. It is during the Ignitions that the Holy Fire flame which lives within each student is brought to life by Spiritual Consciousness. As the Reiki Master facilitating the Ignition process, your responsibility is to create and hold, both the intention and space, for the three different Ignitions to take place.

The three different ignitions are the Pre-Ignition, Master Ignition I, and Master Ignition II. The Pre-ignition is a process of cleansing and preparation for the Student's energy, helping to prepare them mentally, emotionally, physically, and energetically for the Master Ignitions to occur. Because of this, the Pre-ignition must be given within 24-72 hours before the Master Ignitions. This is why it is recommended that Reiki III/ART be taught as the first day of a 3-day Reiki Master workshop, holding the Pre-Ignition at some point during the Level III/ART training day.

Usui Holy Fire Reiki Master can be taught on its own, but you will need to figure out a way to connect with your students to start the ignition process 24-72 hours before the first Usui Holy Fire Reiki Master Ignition.

Meditations vs Guided Experiences

Reiki Master training is a deeply personal experience guided by Spiritual Consciousness, while the Reiki Master holds space. Because of this, meditation is a much bigger part of the training than it is in Levels I-III. In the Outline options provided in this book, you will see recommendations for different guided meditations and experiences to help support you as you hold space for your students.

A guided experience is similar to a guided meditation but is given with the intention to guide the student to connect directly with Spiritual Consciousness, leaving the Reiki Master to simply hold space once the student has connected.

There are scripts included in this book to help you provide the guided experiences, as well as recommendations for which to use at certain points in the process. However, if you are guided to change it up a little or change which guided experience you use, that is ok. Whatever you choose, it is highly recommended that you eventually create your own scripts, using language that is familiar to you.

Usui Holy Fire Reiki Master Pre-Ignition

Preparation for the Pre-Ignition

As part of preparation for an Ignition, it is recommended that you clear the room using the Holy Fire symbol, either before your student arrives, or once their eyes are closed.

For a Usui Holy Fire Ignition, the student can be sitting in a chair, lying on the floor, or in any other comfortable position they choose. Start playing soft meditation music in the background and guide the student to close their eyes and begin focus inward.

You may choose to sit or stand however you like, as long as you are able to hold space both energetically and practically from the position of your choice.

To prepare yourself, begin to flow Reiki. Ask for guidance in setting your ego aside, for any guides you would like to have join you, and set the intention for a Usui Holy Fire Reiki Master Pre-Ignition.

Next, while continuing to flow Reiki, draw Holy Fire over each of your seven major chakras, on both of your palm chakras, and over your entire body from crown to base chakra, remembering to push each symbol in three times.

Usui Holy Fire Reiki Master Pre-Ignition

Below is a script that you can read from or use as a foundation to create your own.

"The Usui Holy Fire Reiki Master Pre-Ignition is a guided experience. For the next few minutes I will be guiding you towards a connection with Spirit. I invite you to follow where you feel led, even if it differs from my guidance. When it is time to return I will call you back to the room.

The Usui Holy Fire Reiki Master Pre-Ignition will begin now.

You find yourself in the middle of a beautiful valley. In front of you there is a forest and all around you there are beautiful mountains reaching high up into the sky. The weather is just perfect, not too hot, not too cold, and you can feel a slight breeze playing upon your skin as the sun warms you. As you look around you, you notice a path laid out before you that leads towards the forest. You begin to follow this path and as you enter the forest you notice the light begins to dim a bit from the tree coverage, and the air gets a bit cooler, and maybe even a bit damp.

(Cont.)

Usui Holy Fire Reiki Master Pre-Ignition

Though you can't explain it, you know you are safe here. That you are being watched over and protected.

You continue down the path and begin to hear the sound of rushing water. As you come around a bend in the path you notice a river off to the right, but decide to keep walking. The further you walk, the louder the sound of the water gets, and you begin to see the path opening up in the distance to what looks like a waterfall.

As you get closer you see the most beautiful waterfall cascading down into a large pool of crystal clear water. At this point you may decide to wade into the water, or you may choose to sit on a rock near the water's edge.

As you begin to relax, enjoying the mist of the waterfall, you notice a bright beam of light coming down from the heavens. The light plays across the water, and eventually finds it's way to you. The light shines on you, through you, surrounds you. Be one with this light and allow it to guide you.

(Cont.)

Usui Holy Fire Reiki Master Pre-Ignition

Stop talking and allow the students to stay in this space for about 20 minutes. Continue to hold space, giving gratitude for the blessings be given, for the opportunity to be a part of something so beautiful and meaningful.

When it is time to return, guide the students back. You may use the following text, or develop your own.

"The Usui Holy Fire Reiki Master Pre-Ignition is now coming to an end. I invite you to begin to feel yourself coming fully back into your body, back into this room. When you are ready, and only when you are ready, I invite you to take a few deep breaths, maybe wiggle your fingers, your toes. And once you feel fully present, I invite you to gently open your eyes. Please take a few moments to reflect on your experience in your journals"

Usui Holy Fire Reiki Master Ignition I

Preparation for the Ignition

As part of preparation for an Ignition, it is recommended that you clear the room using the Holy Fire symbol, either before your student arrives, or once their eyes are closed.

For a Holy Fire Ignition, the student can be sitting in a chair, lying on the floor, or in any other comfortable position they choose. Start playing soft meditation music in the background and guide the student to close their eyes and begin focus inward.

You may choose to sit or stand however you like, as long as you are able to hold space both energetically and practically from the position of your choice.

To prepare yourself, begin to flow Reiki. Ask for guidance in setting your ego aside, for any guides you would like to have join you, and set the intention for a Usui Holy Fire Reiki Master Ignition I.

Next, while continuing to flow Reiki, draw Holy Fire over each of your seven major chakras, on both of your palm chakras, and over your entire body from crown to base chakra, remembering to push each symbol in three times.

Usui Holy Fire Reiki Master Ignition I

Below is a script that you can read from or use as a foundation to create your own.

"For the next few minutes I will be guiding you towards a connection with Spirit. I invite you to follow where you feel led, even if it differs from my guidance. When it is time to return I will call you back to the room.

"Please bring your hands to prayer position, (also known as Gassho position). Take a few nice deep breaths... (give time for a few breaths)... finding yourself feeling centered and calm, begin to flow Reiki.

Focus on the space between your palms, on the energy that flows there. If your thoughts begin to drift, gently brush them aside, and return your attention to the space between your palms (give a few moments here).

A beautiful light begins to descend down from the heavens, flowing between your palms and into your heart. This is the gift of love, of Holy Fire Reiki. Be one with this energy and allow it to guide you"

(Cont.)

Usui Holy Fire Reiki Master Ignition I

Stop talking and allow the students to stay in this space for about 20minutes. Continue to hold space, giving gratitude for the blessings be given, for the opportunity to be a part of something so beautiful and meaningful.

When it is time to return, guide the students back. You may use the following text, or develop your own.

"The Holy Fire Reiki Master Ignition I is now coming to an end. I invite you to begin to feel yourself coming fully back into your body, back into this room. When you are ready, and only when you are ready, I invite you to take a few deep breaths, maybe wiggle your fingers, your toes. And once you feel fully present, I invite you to gently open your eyes. Please take a few moments to reflect on your experience in your journals"

Usui Holy Fire Reiki Master Ignition II

Preparation for the Ignition

As part of preparation for an Ignition, it is recommended that you clear the room using the Holy Fire symbol, either before your student arrives, or once their eyes are closed.

For a Holy Fire Ignition, the student can be sitting in a chair, lying on the floor, or in any other comfortable position they choose. Start playing soft meditation music in the background and guide the student to close their eyes and begin focus inward.

You may choose to sit or stand however you like, as long as you are able to hold space both energetically and practically from the position of your choice.

To prepare yourself, begin to flow Reiki. Ask for guidance in setting your ego aside, for any guides you would like to have join you, and set the intention for a Holy Fire Reiki Master Ignition II.

Next, while continuing to flow Reiki, draw Holy Fire over each of your seven major chakras, on both of your palm chakras, and over your entire body from crown to base chakra, remembering to push each symbol in three times.

Holy Fire Reiki Master Ignition II

Below is a script that you can read from or use as a foundation to create your own.

"For the next few minutes I will be guiding you towards a connection with Spirit. I invite you to follow where you feel led, even if it differs from my guidance. When it is time to return I will call you back to the room.

"Please bring your hands to prayer position, (also known as Gassho position). Take a few nice deep breaths... (give time for a few breaths)... finding yourself feeling centered and calm, begin to flow Reiki.

Focus on the space between your palms, on the energy that flows there. If your thoughts begin to drift, gently brush them aside, and return your attention to the space between your palms. (give a few moments here)

A beautiful light begins to descend down from the heavens, flowing between your palms and into your heart. This is the gift of love, of Holy Fire Reiki. Be one with this energy and allow it to guide you"

(Cont.)

Holy Fire Reiki Master Ignition II

Stop talking and allow the students to stay in this space for about 20minutes. Continue to hold space, giving gratitude for the blessings be given, for the opportunity to be a part of something so beautiful and meaningful.

When it is time to return, guide the students back. You may use the following text, or develop your own.

"The Holy Fire Reiki Master Ignition II is now coming to an end. I invite you to begin to feel yourself coming fully back into your body, back into this room. When you are ready, and only when you are ready, I invite you to take a few deep breaths, maybe wiggle your fingers, your toes. And once you feel fully present, I invite you to gently open your eyes. Please take a few moments to reflect on your experience in your journals"

Chapter 4

The Basics of Teaching Reiki

"Teachers change the world, one heart at a time"

This section covers the basics of teaching Reiki and what you'll need to get started. If you would like more in-depth guidance, additional class outlines, information to help teach Reiki online, additional meditation scripts, etc., please consider Dr. Campbell's book "Teach Reiki Your Way".

Teaching Tips & Tidbits

- ✱ Your #1 job is to hold space – that means creating a container that helps the students to feel safe and secure for what will take place, physically, psychologically, and spiritually.
- ✱ Be prepared to teach, and know that nothing is ever perfect, something will most likely go wonky, and that is OK. Rely on your training, not just the plan, and trust in the fact that you are never alone when teaching Reiki, Spirit is always there to support you.
- ✱ No one knows you "messed up" until you tell them.
- ✱ Providing the opportunity to journal and share can be just as important as the meditative experience itself.
- ✱ Be careful not to place a value on someone's share. Instead of saying that someone's experience was "good" or "bad", try statements like "How interesting" or "What a unique experience" or "Thank you for sharing".
- ✱ Things will shift and you may need to adjust your class schedule… choose what your priorities are in advance, so if this happens you know what to "let go of" easily. For example: If you are short on time, you can skip or skim through certain sections in the book because they can read that on their own later, but they won't always have the teacher around or be able to practice on another person.

* Let them know they will have journaling time after the meditation/experience for 5-10 min. You don't need to actually give them that amount of time exactly, but it helps them know they have time to more deeply explore what may have come up. After about 5 minutes look to see where they are at, and if everyone is done early you can end the time early. If not, a tip for ending gently is to give a heads up a couple minutes before… "So we'll journal for just a couple more minutes…" and then when you are ready to end journaling "I invite you to find a comfortable place to stop and bring your attention back to the group".

Setting Your Fees

Setting your fees for classes depends on many different factors, including your background and level of experience, the location of your classes, what will be included in the experience (materials, extra services, etc.), and the layout/timeline you decide to use to deliver the information.

A good way to create a baseline price is to do an internet search for teachers, wellness centers or other professional organizations in your area and set your prices in a way that aligns with theirs. If you plan to offer something additional in your classes, or bring something unique that people would normally pay extra for, don't be afraid to charge a little more.

Remember, they aren't paying for your time, they are paying for the training and experience you have, and you deserve to be compensated for your knowledge and efforts, and so do your peers. Please remember that when you charge too little, you not only hurt yourself by disrespecting the time and effort you put into your offerings, but you also undercut the Reiki community.

That being said, Reiki is about sharing love and if you feel guided to gift a few seats in your classes, or give discounts to specific students, there is nothing wrong with that. Find what works best for you, and if all else fails, reach out to a few other Reiki Masters and see what they recommend.

Finding Class Space

There are several different options for where to hold your class, and it really comes down to the experience you want to provide. Typical Reiki classes have anywhere from 3 to 15 students, so the space you choose should be able to accommodate the class size you are expecting, including chairs in a circle and tables for practice (1 table for every 3 students is ideal). Most Reiki Masters rent space for their classes from wellness centers, metaphysical stores, or yoga studios, which not only provides space but often marketing which is especially helpful if you are a newer teacher. Pricing can range from $100/day to $500+/day, depending on your location and the type of space you are renting. If you are trying to save a little money and don't need the marketing help those types of places will bring you, try exploring other wellness-oriented businesses that often close on the weekend and might have group space (e.g., therapist offices, chiropractors, or even local colleges).

Allow yourself to think outside the box, take your time and find the right space for you and your students. Meditate with Reiki and ask for guidance, pay attention to synchronicities, and connect with your community for anything they might know of.

Equipment Needed

The following items are recommended with notations on which are optional:

* Class manuals – 1 per student, plus 1 extra (always have an extra!) Dr. Campbell's Reiki manuals for Levels I&II, as well as this manual for Level III/Master, are available online. Bulk order discounts are available by contacting her team online at www.EnergeticPsyche.com

* Reiki Tables* – 1 per every 3 students (12 students = 4 tables, 9 students = 3 tables, 7 students = 3 tables, 4 students = 2 tables). Simple massage tables can be found online ranging from $75-$300+. The less expensive tables are typically lighter and easier to move, just ensure the weight limit and width/length will be appropriate for most students.

* Flat sheet (twin size) or blanket - one per table

* Pillows (for head), blankets* (for comfort or use as a pillow), bolsters* (for under knees) – all optional BUT highly recommended.

* Portable speaker* to play music during meditations. It is highly recommended NOT to use your phone as a speaker.

* Printed and signed certificates – 1 per student and 1 blank just in case there is a spelling error. (Templates are included with the class outlines in the next section of this book)

* Quartz Crystal point in small drawstring bag – 1 per student (optional, but highly recommended if using Dr. Campbell's manual)

* Colored pencils - 1 set per student (optional)

* Journal - 1 per student (optional)

*note that if you rent space from a yoga studio or other wellness space, some of these items may be included in the rental rate, saving you from having to buy and transport them yourself.

Websites & Marketing

Depending on whether you plan to teach primarily online or in-person will make a world of difference when deciding how to market your classes. Some teachers go the route of the internet, working to create a large online presence and gather students for their classes that way. Others put their efforts into marketing to their local community, and many do both. Whatever you choose, just be sure that it is in alignment with who you are. It is completely ok to do a bit of market research and apply techniques you see others using, but remember to honor who you are as a teacher and share your offerings in accordance with that.

Websites and online media management can be costly, whether you do it yourself or hire out, remember that even if you don't pay for it with cash money, you are still paying for it with your time. Having an online presence is helpful, especially as a place for people to come back to you over and over, as most Reiki classes tend to be $200+ some people need time to make their decision, and the info you provide online can be a place they can visit on their own time to help become more informed and comfortable with the idea of becoming a Reiki Practitioner. Just know it can be a simple website, no need to get too fancy, and no matter what, don't let this hold you back from getting started. It is nice to have, but not a "must have".

As awesome as having an online presence is, creating community truly is what matters most (both online and in-person). If you want to market your business you have to meet people beyond more than a "like" and a "follow" online.

Some great ideas to get started include:

- ✱ Schedule time to have coffee/tea with wellness center owners (yoga studios, metaphysical stores, etc.) It can be less intimidating than just walking in and trying to have a conversation in their place of business, plus it gives you an opportunity to get to know each other and who knows, maybe they have been waiting for someone just like you!

* Have a booth at a wellness/holistic fair. You can offer to be a speaker and share about Reiki, market your classes, and offer 10 min chair sessions for $10ea.

* Look up other Reiki Practitioners and wellness-oriented businesses (massage, yoga, chiropractic, acupuncture, etc.) in town and schedule time to chat, either in-person, phone, or video chat. Ask about their offerings and business, who they work with and what their specialties are, and share the same about your business with them. Remember, there is no competition and having others to refer people to when something is outside of your scope is so helpful.

Remember that not everyone you meet is going to be a friend or interested in what you have to offer, and that is OK. Again, those meant for you will find you. Be gentle with yourself, only go where it feels right, and trust that things will align in the best interest of you and your students.

Insurance

Insurance is recommended if you are going to be working with others in a professional capacity. It isn't very expensive, around $100/year, and there are multiple options online for you to choose from. It provides peace of mind for you and shows those you choose to work with that you are serious about your business. It is also helpful to have if you plan to rent space, as many wellness centers, yoga studios, and holistic fairs require it.

Class Registration & Enrollment

Class registration and enrollment can be as simple or as complicated as you want it to be. There are many wonderful CRM (Customer Relationship Management) platforms out there to help you manage your customer interactions, including registration for events. If your business isn't quite ready for a CRM, you can use an online event registration service, like Eventbrite, or even keep it old school, and just make a list.

One big benefit of the online programs is that little to no effort is required from you once you put in all the information and get it set up. However, most programs require a fee or percentage of your sales, and many Reiki teachers like to have some level of control regarding who is joining their classes, which is difficult with an online auto-registration system. A nice in-between is to have an automated system (like Calendly or Acuity) so interested students can schedule a call with you. From that point on you can enter them into your CRM or add them to your student list, it's up to you.

Just one note on all of this… sometimes these systems seem to make things MORE complicated than they need to be, so if it isn't for you, then it isn't for you. None of this is necessary to be successful as a Reiki Practitioner or Teacher, but it might be helpful. You are the only one who will be able to decide what is right for your business.

Appendix A

Reiki Symbols

Reiki Level II Symbols

Choku Rei

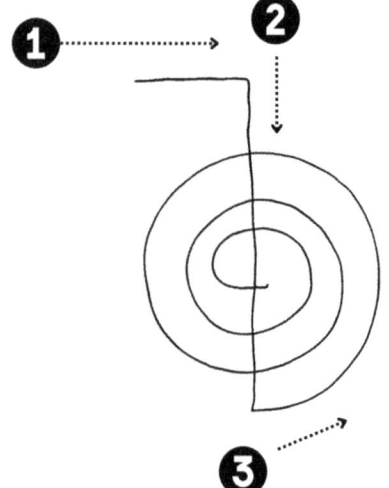

Sei Heki

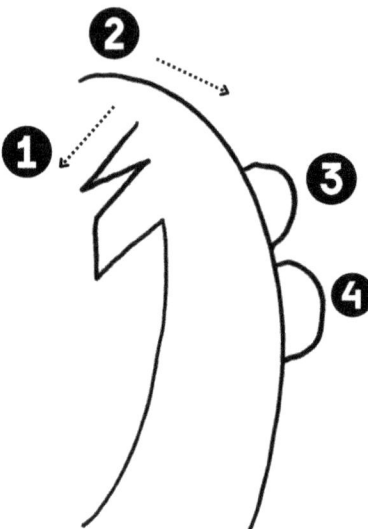

Hon Sha Ze Sho Nen

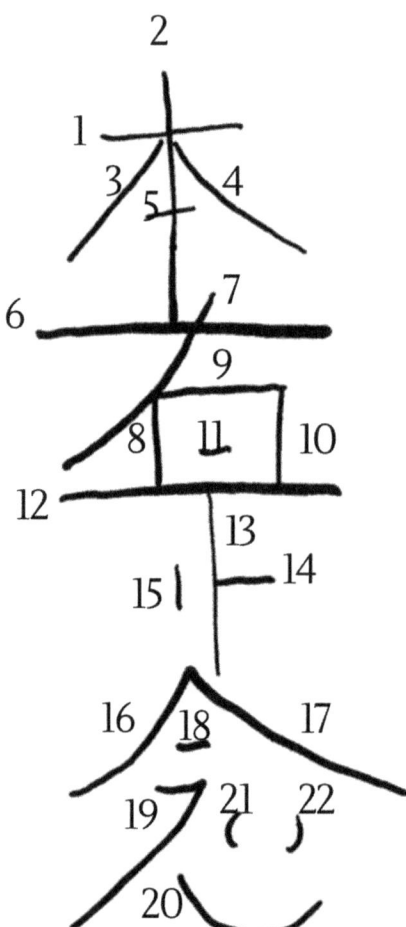

Choku Rei

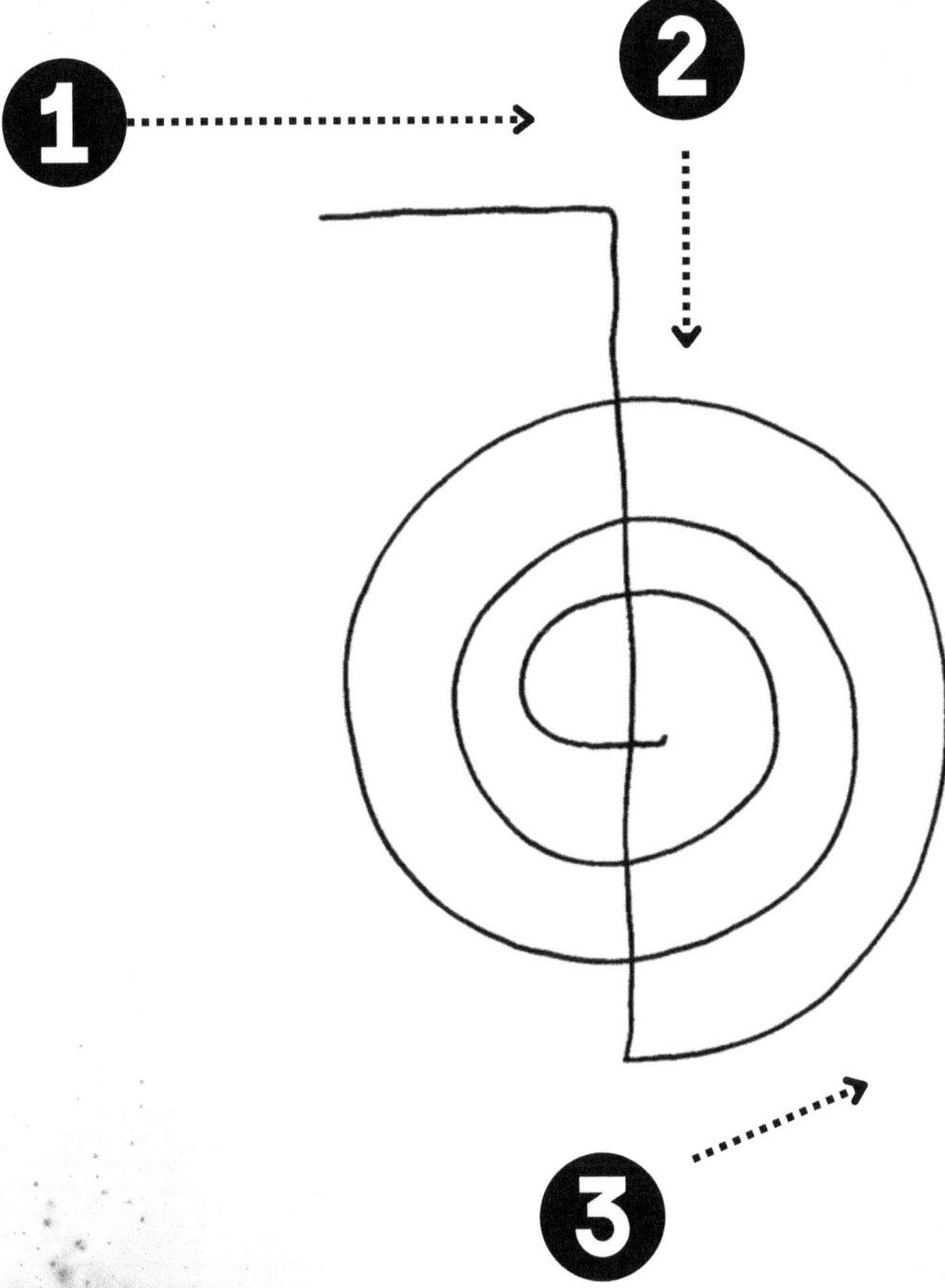

Sei Heki

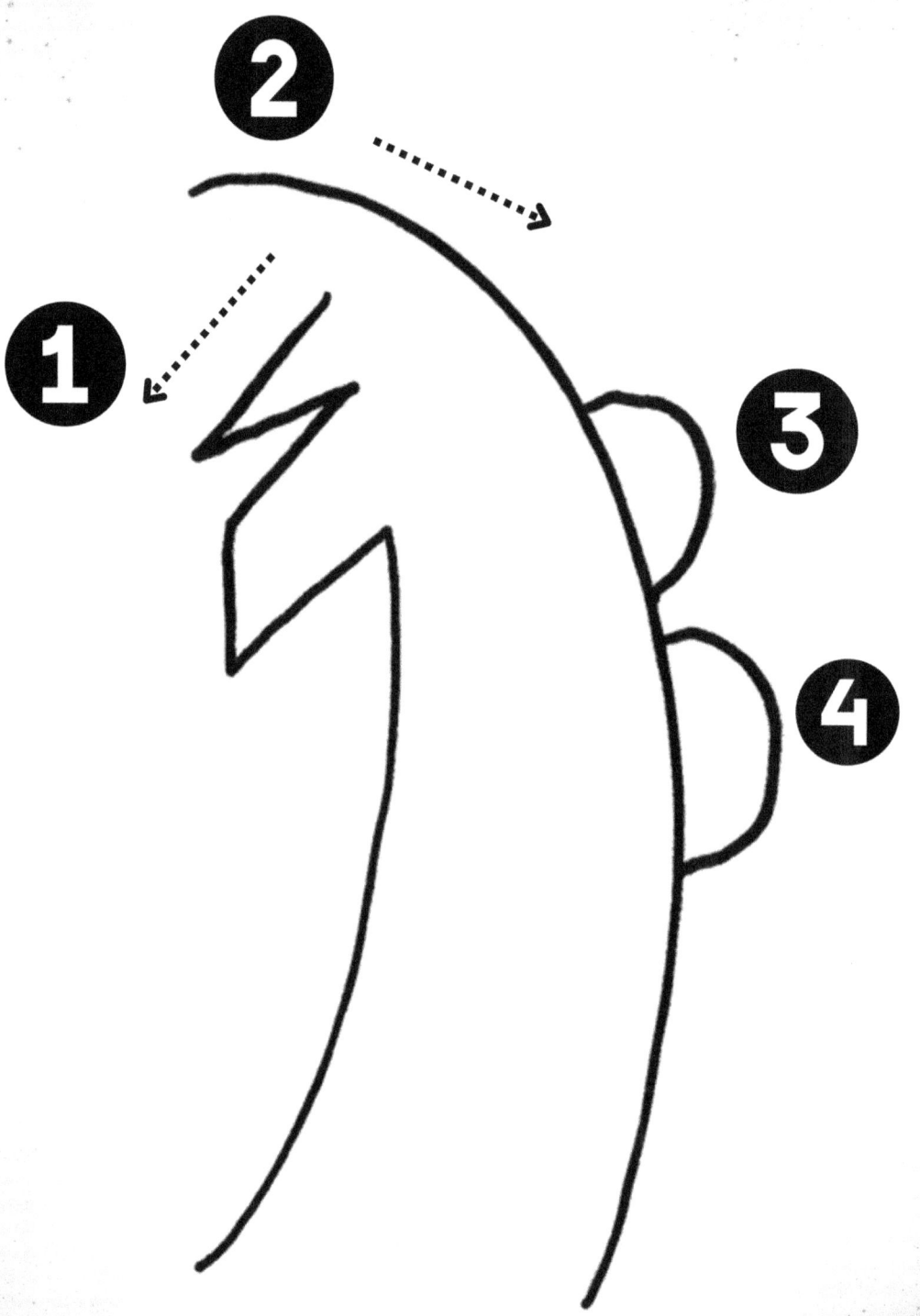

Hon Sha Ze Sho Nen

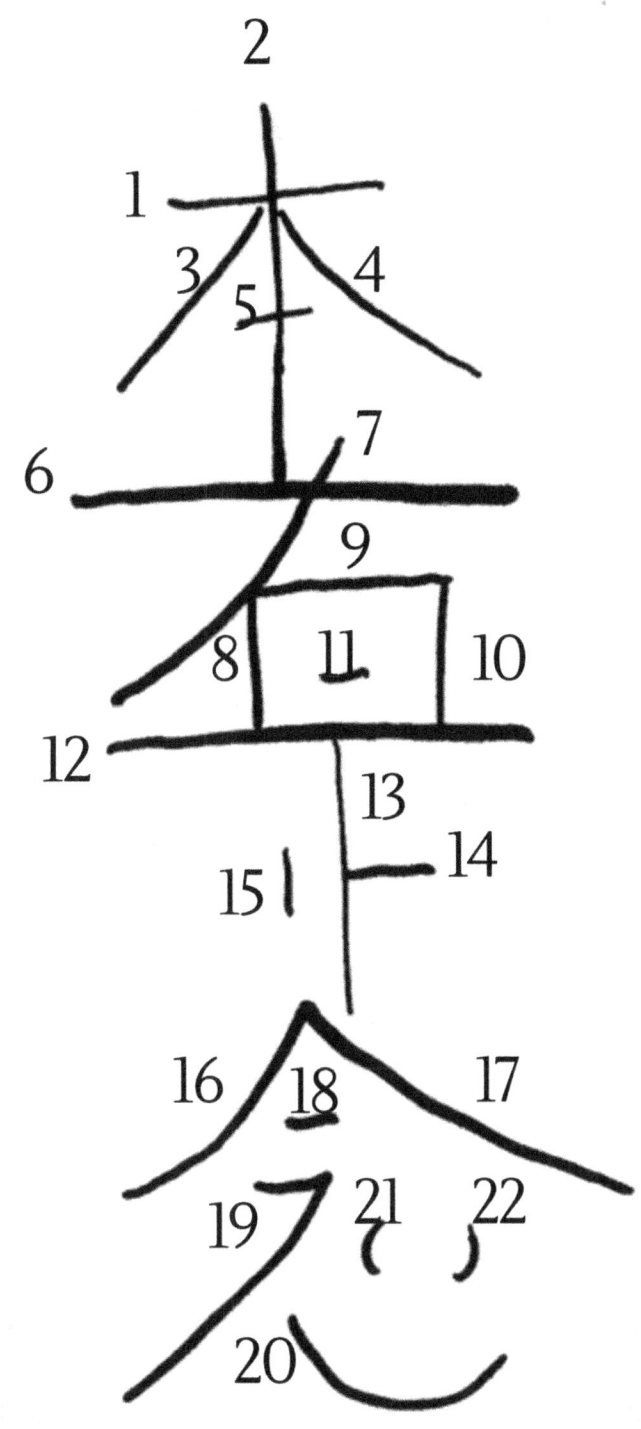

Dai Ko Myo

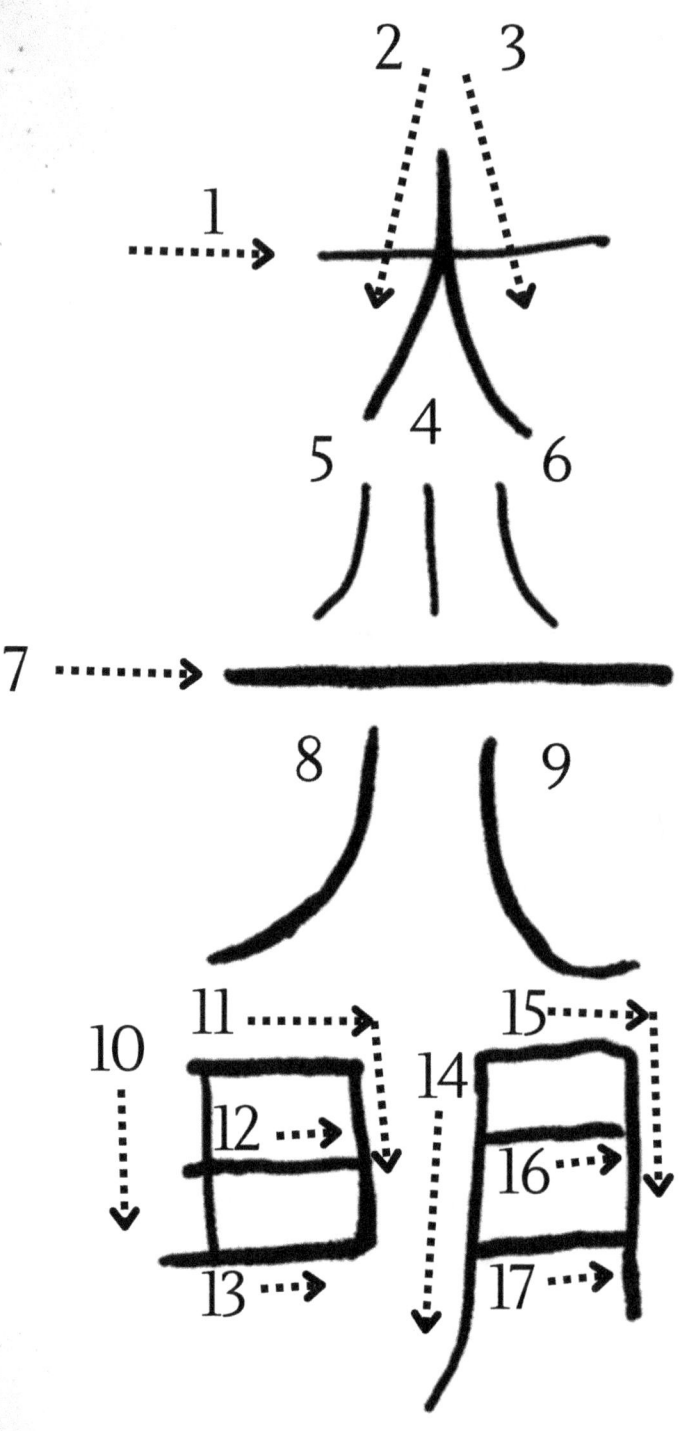

Holy Fire

Appendix B

Reiki Class Outlines

Standard Reiki Class Outlines

The following class outlines are considered "standard" because they are currently the most commonly offered layouts for Reiki classes, but that doesn't mean they are the ONLY way to teach Reiki. They are provided as guidance to help create a strong foundation for you to grow from. If you are interested in other options check out Dr. Campbell's book, "Teach Reiki your Way".

Each class includes the bare minimum required to be considered a "certificate course". As mentioned previously, many teachers opt to add in more material, just keep in mind if you delete any of the fundamentals you risk straying away from teaching a "Reiki" class. This is OK, Dr. Campbell herself has created multiple courses that include Reiki attunements but don't certify individuals to become practitioners. Just be sure that you are clear about what you are providing your students, so they don't think they are getting certified as practitioners, if they aren't.

Also included is a template for a prep email to be sent out to your students at least one week in advance of the class, to help them prepare, as well as certificate templates for Level I - Master.

It is recommended that you use the provided outlines and templates as a foundation to create your own materials which will include the elements that truly make the class yours.

The chapters and meditations listed are referencing information from Dr. Campbell's Reiki class manuals "Learn to Practice Reiki", "Become a Reiki Master". and "Teach Reiki Your Way".

Class Prep Email

Greetings,

I'm excited to share the magic of Reiki with you this Weekend! Below is some info to help you prepare for the class.

Note: I need you to email me back with the name you want on your certificate by (enter date here).

Class Date:
Location:
Time:

A few bits of guidance...

- Please bring a journal or notebook and something to write with. I invite you to bring a highlighter or tabs, as well as colored pencils/crayons/markers for any journaling we do after our meditations.
- Dress comfortably, and feel free to bring fluffy socks or a blanket.
- You are invited to use meditation cushions, or things of that nature to sit on/with. (Let them know here if you will be sitting at desks/tables or if you will be sitting on the floor/in a chair). Please bring anything you would like to make your time more comfortable.
- There are no planned breaks, but I usually try to take one every hour or so, or as needed. And there will be a break for lunch, but no set time.
- Hot/cold filtered water is available, bring a water bottle if you'd like.

Standard Class Prep Email (cont.)

- Lunch will be 45-60ish minutes, feel free to bring your lunch to enjoy in the studio (no fridge FYI), and there are also quite a few places in town that you can grab something from if you'd prefer that.

- To physically prepare: do your best to abstain from, or minimize alcohol, meat products, caffeine, and maintain a "clean" diet. Not a requirement, just do what feels right for your body. Please be sure to do your best to get a good night's sleep before class.

- To mentally prepare: try to spend some time in meditation every day, play attention to your dreams, and any other synchronicities that might occur.

If you have any other questions please let me know. My cell is (Phone number here) in case you need to text/call me. I am looking forward to our class together.

See you Saturday!

(Your Name here)

Usui Reiki Level I
Class Outline (8hrs)

- Logistics & Safety: Share start/end time of class, break policy, location of restrooms/exits/water. (5min)
- Review of materials needed for class: (5min)
    - Class manual: "Learn to Practice Reiki" (have them write their name inside)
    - Journal/something to write in & with
- Intros – Ask students to share their name, any experience with energy healing, and their expectations for the class (20-30min)
- Share your Reiki story with the students (5-10min)
- Holy Love Guided Experience - Winding River, journaling & share (15-30min)
- Chapter 1: Getting to Know the Energetic Body (60min)
- Chapter 2: Understanding Reiki Energy (60min)
- Chapter 3: Energy Healing Techniques (60min)

Lunch (30-60min)

- Level 1 Attunement, journaling & share (30-60min)
- Practice flowing Reiki as a group with hands in prayer (Gassho) position (10-15min)

Usui Reiki Level I
Class Outline (cont.)

- Guide students through practice of a self-healing using standard hand placements, journaling, group share (30-45min)
- Hand out certificates
- Closing meditation of your choice.

Notes:

Times listed are approximate and will vary based on number of students and the questions asked. When you take lunch will vary on your start/end time but is suggested before or after Chapter 3 if possible.

Usui Holy Fire Reiki Ryoho

First Degree Reiki

This is to Verify that

Has received the necessary attunement and knowledge of the Usui Holy Fire Reiki System of healing and now has the basic requirements to administer hands-on healing through the transmission of spiritually guided life force energy for First Degree Usui Holy Fire Reiki.

_____   _____
Date of Completion   Reiki Master Teacher

Usui Reiki Level II
Class Outline (8hrs)

- Logistics & Safety: Share start/end time of class, break policy, location of restrooms/exits/water. (5min)
- Review of materials needed for class: (5min)
- Class manual: "Learn to Practice Reiki" (have them write their name inside)
- Quartz crystal in bag
- Journal/something to write in & with
- Intros – Ask students to share their name, any experience with energy healing, and their expectations for the class (20-30min)
- Share your Reiki story with the students (5-10min)
- Holy Love Guided Experience - Waterfall, journaling & share (15-30min)
- Chapter 4: The Healing Power of Crystals (30-60min)
- Chapter 5: Using Reiki Energy with Others (30min)
- Chapter 6: Usui Holy Fire Reiki Level II Symbols (60min)

Lunch & Symbol Practice (60min)

Usui Reiki Level II Class Outline (cont.)

- Level II Symbol "Test" (30min)
- Level II Attunement, Journaling & Share (30-60min)
- Practice giving Reiki in groups of 2-4. Start with Reiki & no symbols, and then add symbols to note the difference (60min)
- Guide students through a distance Reiki session (20min)
- Guide students through using Choku Rei to seal and clear the space (15min)
- Chapter 7: Working with Reiki in Everyday life (60min)
- Practice in groups of 2-4 using guide from Ch.7 on giving a "Complete Reiki Session" (60min)
- Chapter 8: Doing Business as a Reiki Practitioner (optional)
- Hand out Certificates
- Closing meditation of your choice

Notes:

Times listed are approximate and will vary based on number of students and the questions asked. When you take lunch will vary on your start/end time, but should occur before the attunement.

Usui Holy Fire Reiki Ryoho
Second Degree Reiki

This is to Verify that

Has received the necessary attunement and knowledge of the Usui Holy Fire Reiki System of healing and now has the basic requirements to administer hands-on and distant healing through the transmission of spiritually guided life force energy for Second Degree Usui Holy Fire Reiki.

_____
Reiki Master Teacher

_____
Date of Completion

Usui Reiki Level I/II
Class Outline (2 Days)

Day one:

- Logistics & Safety: Share start/end time of class, break policy, location of restrooms/exits/water. (5min)
- Review of materials needed for class: (5min)
  - Class manual: "Learn to Practice Reiki" (have them write their name inside)
  - Quartz crystal in bag
  - Journal/something to write in & with
- Intros – Ask students to share their name, any experience with energy healing, and their expectations for the class (20-30min)
- Share your Reiki story with the students (5-10min)
- Holy Love Guided Experience - Winding River, journaling & share (15-30min)
- Chapter 1: Getting to Know the Energetic Body (60min)

Usui Reiki Level I/II Class Outline (cont.)

Day one (cont.)

- Chapter 2: Understanding Reiki Energy (60min)
- Chapter 3: Energy Healing Techniques (60min)

    Lunch (30-60min)

- Level 1 Attunement, Journaling, & Share (30-60min)
- Practice flowing Reiki as a group with hands in prayer (Gassho) position (10-15min)
- Guide students through practice of a self-healing using standard hand placements, journaling, group share (30-45min)
- Provide students with a copy of the level II symbols, briefly explaining each one and that they will need to verbally name and draw each one by memory the following day.
- Closing meditation of your choice.

<u>Notes</u>:
Times listed are approximate and will vary based on number of students and the questions asked. When you take lunch will vary on your start/end time but is suggested before or after Chapter 3 if possible.

Usui Reiki Level I/II Class Outline (cont.)

Day Two

- Check-in with students - How is everyone feeling? Any questions come up overnight?
- Holy Love Guided Experience - Waterfall, journaling & share (15-30min)
- Chapter 4: The Healing Power of Crystals (30-60min)
- Chapter 5: Using Reiki Energy with Others (30min)
- Chapter 6: Usui Holy Fire Reiki Level II Symbols (60min)

    Lunch & Symbol Practice (60min)

- Level II Symbol "Test" (30min)
- Level I1 Attunement, journaling, & share (30-60min)
- Practice giving Reiki in groups of 2-4. Start with Reiki & no symbols, and then add symbols to note the difference (60min)

Usui Reiki Level I/II Class Outline (cont.)

Day Two (cont.)

- Guide students through a distance Reiki session (20min)
- Guide students through using Choku Rei to seal and clear the space. (15min)
- Chapter 7: Working with Reiki in Everyday life (60min)
- Practice in groups of 2-4 using guide from Ch.7 on giving a "Complete Reiki Session" (60min)
- Chapter 8: Doing Business as a Reiki Practitioner (optional)
- Hand out certificates
- Closing meditation of your choice

Notes:

Times listed are approximate and will vary based on number of students and the questions asked. When you take lunch will vary on your start/end time, but should occur before the attunement.

Usui Holy Fire Reiki Ryoho
First & Second Degree Reiki

This is to Verify that

Has received the necessary attunements and knowledge of the Usui Holy Fire Reiki System of healing and now has the basic requirements to administer hands-on and distant healing through the transmission of spiritually guided life energy for First and Second Degree Usui Holy Fire Reiki.

Date of Completion

Reiki Master Teacher

Usui Holy Fire Reiki Level III/ART Class Outline (8hrs)

- Logistics & Safety: Share start/end time of class, break policy, location of restrooms/exits/water. (5min)
- Review of materials needed for class: (5min)
    - Reiki manual (have them write their name inside)
    - Quartz crystal in bag
    - Journal/Something to write in & with
- Intros – Ask students to share their name, what energy healing training they have, and their expectations for the class (20-30min)
- Share your Reiki story with the students (5-10min)
- Holy Love Guided Experience - Winding River, journaling & share (15-30min)
- Chapter 1: Setting a Foundation (30min)
- Chapter 2: Reiki Level III/Art (30min)
- Chapter 2: ... The Healing Power of Crystals Crystals (30min)

Usui Reiki Level III/ART Class Outline (cont.)

- Chapter 2: ... Exploring the Chakra System (30min)
- Chapter 2: ... Reiki Master Symbol (20min)

Lunch & Symbol Practice (60min)

- Dai Ko Myo Symbol "Test"
- Chapter 2: ... Understanding Attunements (30-60min)
- Attunement to Dai Ko Myo, journaling & share (30-60min)
- Demonstrate a Healing Attunement (10min)
- Practice in groups 2-3 giving each other Healing Attunements (30-60min)
- Hand out certificates
- Closing meditation of your choice

Notes:
Times listed are approximate and will vary based on number of students and the questions asked.

Usui Holy Fire Reiki Ryoho
Level III / ART

This is to Verify that

Has received the necessary attunement and knowledge for the Advanced Reiki Training Level of the Usui Holy Fire system of healing, and has demonstrated comprehension of its principles and proficiency.

_____
Reiki Master Teacher

_____
Date of Completion

Usui Holy Fire Reiki Level III/ART & Reiki Master Class Outline (3 days)

Day One

- Logistics & Safety: Share start/end time of class, break policy, location of restrooms/exits/water. (5min)
- Review of materials needed for class: (5min)
    - Class manuals: "Learn to Practice Reiki", "Become a Reiki Master", and optionally "Teach Reiki Your Way" (have them write their name inside each)
    - Quartz crystal in bag
    - Journals/something to write in & with
- Intros – Ask students to share their name, what energy healing training they have, and their expectations for the class (20-30min)
- Share your Reiki story with the students (5-10min)
- Holy Love Guided Experience - Winding River, journaling & share (15-30min)
- Chapter 1: Setting a Foundation (30min)

Usui Holy Fire Reiki Level III/ART & Reiki Master Class Outline

Day One (cont.)

- Chapter 2: Reiki Level III/Art (30min)
- Chapter 2: ... The Healing Power of Crystals Crystals (30min)
- Chapter 2: ... Exploring the Chakra System (30min)
- Chapter 2: ... Reiki Master Symbol (20min)

Lunch & Symbol Practice (60min)

- Dai Ko Myo Symbol "test"
- Usui Holy Fire Reiki Master Pre-Ignition
- Chapter 2: ... Understanding Attunements (30-60min)
- Attunement to Dai Ko Myo, journaling & share (30-60min)

Usui Holy Fire Reiki Level III/ART & Reiki Master Class Outline

Day One (cont.)

- Demonstrate a Healing Attunement (10min)
- Practice in groups 2-3 giving each other Healing Attunements and have each student create their own "Quick Guide"(45-60min)
- Closing meditation of your choice

Usui Holy Fire Reiki Level III/ART & Reiki Master Class Outline

Day Two

- Check-in with students - How is everyone feeling? Any questions come up overnight? (30-60min)
- Holy Love Experience - Winding River, journaling & share (15-30min)
- Chapter 3: ... Becoming a Reiki Master (10min)
- Chapter 3: ... Usui Holy Fire Reiki & Holy Fire Symbol (20min)
- Usui Holy Fire Reiki Master Ignition I, journaling & share (30-45min)
- Chapter 3: ... Reiki Level I, II, III/ART Attunements (15-30min) (Skip Usui Holy Fire Reiki Master Ignitions for now)

Lunch (60min)

- Practice in groups 2-3 giving each other Healing Attunements using Holy Fire and have each student create their own "Quick Guide" (60min)

Usui Holy Fire Reiki Level III/ART & Reiki Master Class Outline

Day Two (cont.)

- Demonstrate a Reiki Level I Attunement (10min)
- Practice in groups 2-3 giving each other Reiki Level I Attunements and have each student create their own "Quick Guide" (60min)
- Closing meditation of your choice.

Note:

If you have extra time, feel free to move into Level II Attunements.

Usui Holy Fire Reiki Level III/ART & Reiki Master Class Outline

Day Three

- Check-in with students - How is everyone feeling? Any questions come up overnight? (30-60min)
- Usui Holy Fire Reiki Master Ignition II, journaling & share (30-45min)
- Demonstrate a Reiki Level II Attunement and have each student create their own "Quick Guide" (10min)
- Practice in groups 2-3 giving each other Reiki Level II Attunements and have each student create their own "Quick Guide" (30-45min)
- Demonstrate a Reiki Level III Attunement (10min)
- Practice in groups 2-3 giving each other Reiki Level III Attunements and have each student create their own "Quick Guide" (30-45min)

Lunch (60min)

Usui Holy Fire Reiki Level III/ART & Reiki Master Class Outline

Day Three (cont.)

- Chapter 3: ... Usui Holy Fire Reiki Master Ignitions (30min)
- Chapter 4: Teaching Reiki (Option to move into Dr. Campbell's teaching guide, "Teach Reiki Your Way" or stay in "Become a Reiki Master") (60-120min)
- Hand out certificates
- Closing meditation of your choice

Note:

Times listed are approximate and will vary based on number of students and the questions asked.

Holy Fire Reiki Master can be taught as a standalone 2-day course, however, you must somehow give the Holy Fire Reiki Master Pre-ignition to the students within 72 hours of the first Master Ignition.

Usui Holy Fire Reiki Ryoho
Level III/ART & Reiki Master

This is to Verify that

Has received the necessary attunements and knowledge of Advanced Reiki Training and the Master level of the Usui Holy Fire system of healing, and has demonstrated comprehension of its principles and proficiency in the giving of all attunements and now has the basic requirements necessary to teach all levels of the Usui Holy Fire Reiki system of healing as a free and independent Reiki master.

_____
Reiki Master Teacher

_____
Date of Completion

Appendix C

Guided Meditations & Experiences

Holy Love Experience – Winding River

You find yourself in the middle of a beautiful valley. In front of you there is a forest and all around you there are beautiful mountains reaching high up into the sky. The weather is just perfect, not too hot, not too cold, and you can feel a slight breeze playing upon your skin as the sun warms you. As you look around you, you notice a path laid out before you that leads towards the forest. You begin to follow this path and as you enter the forest you notice the light begins to dim a bit from the tree coverage, and the air gets a bit cooler, and maybe even a bit damp.

Though you can't explain it, you know you are safe here. That you are being watched over and protected.

You continue down the path and begin to hear the sound of rushing water. As you come around a bend in the path you notice a river off to the right.

Holy Love Experience – Winding River (cont.)

You begin to walk down towards the river, and once you get to the river's edge you notice a bright beam of sunlight shining down from the sky, reflecting gently across the water. As you look into the light, you realize this is no normal beam of light, but rather a light that is shining down from the highest of heavens, just for you. Take a few moments here to allow yourself to receive whatever guidance this light has for you.

(Stop talking and allow the students to stay in this space for about 10-15 min. When it is time to return, guide the students back.

I invite you to begin to feel yourself coming fully back into your body, back into this room. When you are ready, and only when you are ready, I invite you to take a few deep breaths, maybe wiggle your fingers, your toes. And once you feel fully present, I invite you to gently open your eyes. Please take a few moments to reflect on your experience in your journals.

Holy Love Experience – Waterfall

You find yourself in the middle of a beautiful valley. In front of you there is a forest and all around you there are beautiful mountains reaching high up into the sky. The weather is just perfect, not too hot, not too cold, and you can feel a slight breeze playing upon your skin as the sun warms you. As you look around you, you notice a path laid out before you that leads towards the forest. You begin to follow this path and as you enter the forest you notice the light begins to dim a bit from the tree coverage, and the air gets a bit cooler, and maybe even a bit damp.

Though you can't explain it, you know you are safe here. That you are being watched over and protected.

You continue down the path and begin to hear the sound of rushing water. As you come around a bend in the path you notice a river off to the right, but decide to keep walking.

Holy Love Experience – Waterfall (cont.)

The further you walk, the louder the sound of the water gets, and you begin to see the path opening up in the distance to what looks like a waterfall.

As you get closer you see the most beautiful waterfall cascading down into a large pool of crystal clear water. At this point you may decide to wade into the water, or you may choose to sit on a rock near the water's edge.

As you begin to relax, enjoying the mist of the waterfall, you notice a bright beam of light coming down from the heavens. The light plays across the water, and eventually finds it's way to you. The light shines on you, through you, surrounds you. Be one with this light and allow it to guide you.

Stop talking and allow the students to stay in this space for about 10-15 minutes.

Holy Love Experience – Waterfall (cont.)

When it is time to return, guide the students back.

I invite you to begin to feel yourself coming fully back into your body, back into this room. When you are ready, and only when you are ready, I invite you to take a few deep breaths, maybe wiggle your fingers, your toes. And once you feel fully present, I invite you to gently open your eyes. Please take a few moments to reflect on your experience in your journals.